RECAP

About the Author

Kevin Cardiff is the former Secretary-General in Ireland's Department of Finance and is currently a member of the European Court of Auditors. He lives in Luxembourg.

The views expressed in this book are the author's own and not necessarily those of any organisation he has been associated with.

All author royalties from the sale of this book will be donated to charity.

RECAP

Inside Ireland's Financial Crisis

Kevin Cardiff

The Liffey Press

Published by
The Liffey Press Ltd
Raheny Shopping Centre, Second Floor
Raheny, Dublin 5, Ireland
www.theliffeypress.com

© 2016 Kevin Cardiff

A catalogue record of this book is
available from the British Library.

ISBN 978-1-908308-82-5

Printed in Spain by GraphyCems.

Contents

To Yvonne

Preface

This book started as a draft statement for the Oireachtas Inquiry into the banking crisis (the Banking Inquiry), and much of it was written, in first draft at least, over the course of Christmas 2014 and Easter 2015 as I prepared for the Inquiry.

It was originally intended for publication in November 2015, after the Banking Inquiry's report had issued. I did not wish to produce any document, other than my formal statement, while the Inquiry was taking evidence, and when I first spoke to a publisher in the Summer of 2015, I made clear that I would not allow any publication date that might influence other witnesses. When the proposed date for the report of the Banking Inquiry was put back to January, the publication of this book was also postponed, as a courtesy to the Inquiry process.

So why not make my statement to the Inquiry and leave it at that? Well, the factual content of this small volume is heavily based on my Banking Inquiry statement, but I felt that in a book one could try to convey something extra – some sense of the atmosphere of the time, of the pressures and incentives affecting decisions taken, of the way people behaved. I think there is some public value in putting my personal perspective on these issues in the public domain.

1

There is to be no personal financial benefit in the exercise. My publisher was kind enough to believe that this book will be 'of keen interest to a particular audience', presumably meaning that you, the reader, are particular and not greatly numerous, so that I need not think I can write a best seller. But apart from some copies of the book to give to family, friends and so forth, any small royalty payments due on foot of this will go straight to charity.

There are some real limitations of which the reader should be aware. First, this book is not a history. It is a personal reflection on historical events in which I was involved. The perspective is mine, and with some limited exceptions I have tried to convey my own recollection of events rather than produce a thorough and complete narrative. I simply do not have the personal distance from the events at this point in time to believe I could do the latter task objectively. Being from my own perspective, it does not agree in every detail with all the others who were witnesses to the same events and who gave their evidence at the Banking Inquiry or in other ways. I have tried in putting together my narrative to recreate the facts as I knew them at the time, but I have not tried to reconcile every difference with others. Still, it should be evident, I hope, that there is a good deal of research behind both this document and my Banking Inquiry evidence.

The book is also not a warts-and-all description of the people I interacted with in four or five awful years. That would not be fair to many good people who I worked with – or against – and who do not deserve to be caricatured or scapegoated, for I am sure that anything positive I might write will be quickly forgotten and that anything negative will be exaggerated. There were very few people I dealt with who were so unpleasant that I would wish on them and their families the kind of personalised attacks that characterise some parts of our modern media and politics, so I am not going to provide the ammunition, even if I am not sure that all of the people concerned would have the same scruples. For legal reasons I also have avoided going into any depth on issues which might become the subject of future trials – the Banking Inquiry was highly constrained in this regard also.

Introduction

I had never been in a full police-escorted convoy before, but I was fairly sure that this was the best-in-class version. I was in a group of three cars, arranged by the Irish Embassy, on the way into Paris. The Taoiseach, Brian Cowen, was in another car, just ahead, with Anne Anderson, the Irish ambassador.

We were on the way to the first ever Eurozone Heads of State and Government Meeting – or in other words, a meeting of the presidents or prime ministers of each of the countries who were members of the single currency, together with the Presidents of the European Commission, Manuel Barroso, and of the European Central Bank, Jean-Claude Trichet. The meeting had been called by President Sarkozy of France, encouraged by some of his colleagues, including in particular the Spanish Prime Minister Zapatero. The agenda for the meeting was to deal with the still unravelling mess that was the banking crisis.

I had taken some papers out of my bag to review on the way into the city from the airport, but it quickly became clear that the journey would be short and fast – the cars seemed to be straining to match the speed of the motor cycle outriders who were providing the escort. They were moving very quickly and every now and then would do a sort of synchronised jink left or right from one lane to another, while the cars continued in the lane they were in. Sirens wailed whenever there was an obstacle, and it was clear that when these guys cleared a route, it was properly cleared.

On arriving on a Parisian side street, we were asked to exit the cars and ushered around a corner into a very crowded little security office, and from there around the edges of a courtyard crammed with journalists.

Meanwhile, the Taoiseach was asked to stay in his car. He was in a queue to be driven in more statesmanlike fashion into the courtyard of the Élysée Palace, HQ of the French President Nicolas Sarkozy, where the President himself was standing on a set of steps in front of the door to the Palace. Around the courtyard were ranged a party of young, tall, blue-uniformed, plumed-helmeted guards, swords held with the hilt at waist height, pointing vertically. It was a very impressive display, imposing a sense of formality and order, and even a little intimidation, on the whole courtyard.

There was behind them a much less orderly scrum of journalists and photographers, and behind them the stream of officials going into the same meeting as the senior politicians, but who were not of course to be formally greeted by Sarkozy. The officials would be held back and kept out of photo-shot as an incoming prime-minister would exit his or her limousine. The prime minister concerned would shake hands with Sarkozy, smile and hold their pose for a few moments to accommodate the photographers, and then be escorted by Sarkozy as far as the door. Sarkozy would then turn back down the steps to await the car carrying the next prime minister.

As he did so, the multinational bevy of officials who had been held back would get the signal to rush for the door, so that as many as possible would enter the building before the passage was again blocked off pending the next prime minister's photo-op with Sarkozy. Just inside the door we had to push our way through earlier arrivers, who had decided to wait right there for their own leader to come in.

It was, for a few minutes, chaotic, and it reflected almost perfectly the situation that we were there to consider – a highly structured and formalised set of banking institutions, still enshrouded in all the granite-buildinged, smart-suited grandeur that they were used to, but inwardly in chaos.

This meeting was to discuss how Europe should solve, or at least address, its banking crisis, and I was there because I worked in the Department of Finance, as head of the Tax and Financial Services Division. For the past year or so, one of my jobs was to watch, report and prepare, as strains on the Irish banking system slowly increased. But for just over a month, I had been engaged, with quite a few others, in trying to cope with a real crisis.

For me, that crisis had broken on Friday 5 September 2008, around 11.00 p.m., when my telephone rang. I listened and spoke quietly, and then I pressed the call complete button. My wife, who was close by, but could not have heard the conversation, nonetheless looked at me and asked a simple question, 'well, which bank is it?' No surprise that my wife was attuned to the possibility of trouble. She knew from my work pattern and body language that something had been brewing, and she remembered the late night phone calls and unusual behaviour patterns that had prevailed in our house for a day or two the previous year, when Northern Rock, a British bank with an Irish branch, was in difficulty.

The telephone call that night was from William Beausang, a very competent colleague who was heading up the secret work we had been doing on banking crisis preparation. He told me that he had heard from the Financial Regulator's office that an incorrect report had been circulated by Reuters about Irish Nationwide Building Society (INBS), and that as a result the Regulator feared a run on the building society's deposit base the following week – they were asking about my availability for a meeting first thing Monday morning.

William and I decided that if there was the potential for a bank 'run' on Monday, then we better get to work – tomorrow. And the planning for such an event envisaged an immediate meeting of the Department of Finance, the Central Bank and the Financial Regulator. I pressed for a meeting the following morning, and a large group of people met around a table that Saturday morning in the Central Bank Building in Dame Street. We probably already knew, in our hearts, that for many of us the meeting that morning was only the start of a series of events that would determine our lives for quite some time to come, and would affect literally millions of people.

In the course of the next week or 10 days, the people in the room and their bosses would decide on the plan for responding to the threat of a run on the building society, refine a plan for nationalising it, develop messages for communicating the news to the public, make arrangements for emergency call centres in Dame Street and in the Department of Finance and engage with the larger banks about their potential role in handling the INBS crisis.

In the next month, the same group of people and a few more would consider the potential for the meltdown of the entire Irish financial system – and not just the Irish one – develop a range of options for decision by the Central Bank and by the Government – not a single one of them attractive – refine the draft legislation to allow for the nationalisation of banks and building societies and the provision of guarantees and capital and liquidity supports, implement a very broad banking guarantee, and present legislation to be passed by the Oireachtas within days of its being announced.

In the seven or eight months from that phone call in Dublin Airport, the Government and the various official parties would have recapitalised most of the domestic banking system, nationalised one bank, fought a sometimes almost clandestine public relations battle with people seeking to undermine the bank guarantee, and planned the formation of the National Asset Management Agency, which would potentially become one of the world's biggest property asset managers.

As tension rose and the stresses of the moment increased, I was proud of my association with many excellent colleagues, who threw themselves wholeheartedly into what we knew was the defence of the economic wellbeing of our country, and disappointed with only a few. Contrary to how they have often been portrayed, the civil servants engaged in this battle generally behaved with competence and skill, assisted by colleagues in other institutions and by various groups of consultants.

As individuals they were generally very capable, but as a group they were lacking in the broad range of skills required for the occasion. The same could be said for almost every civil service in the world, I think – with the possible exception of those which had been through their own financial crises in the previous two decades.

In the UK, in France, in Belgium, in Germany, in the United States, Austria, Luxembourg and other countries, and at the highest decision making levels of the European Union, September and October were months in which unprecedented events led to a raft of apparently 'last ditch' crisis meetings of ministers, heads of state, central bankers, regulators and financial institutions' own directors, often in the dead of night, to create a firewall against the impending financial conflagration.

This is my description of what happened in those times – it is an honest portrayal, I hope. But of course, it is one-sided, being from my perspective only, and the challenges of memory and the need for summarisation means it is necessarily not comprehensive.

1

Crisis Point

So we met on Saturday, 6 September 2008, in a conference room in the Central Bank building in Dublin's Dame Street. I don't remember all the participants, but the room was full, and we set about preparing for the possibility that the Irish Nationwide Building Society, or INBS, would be in serious difficulty that Monday. Staff from the Central Bank, from the Financial Regulator, from the Department of Finance and later the National Treasury Management Agency (NTMA) met together and in smaller groups to prepare different aspects of a crisis response. We considered the time it would take to bring legislation to the Dáil, the steps that could be taken to get more information on INBS, the manner in which members of the public could be kept informed, the infrastructure that would be required to deal with hundreds or thousands of phone calls from concerned members of the public – and approaches were prepared in relation to all of these matters.

Of course, this was not the first time any of these issues had been considered. Work had been ongoing for months on crisis preparation, on approaches that might be taken, on developing legislation. Officials in the Office of the Parliamentary Counsel – the lawyers who draft legislation for the Government – and the Attorney General's office had been advising

11

the Department of Finance on legislation and state aids matters, and a draft Bill was well advanced.

But now we were coming close to being asked to put the theory into practice, and the preparatory work was paying off. But at the end of that Saturday's work, with quite a lot achieved but enormous work still to be done, I announced that of course we would be continuing our work the following day, and I was a bit surprised by the body language in the room, a distinct lack of enthusiasm for my demand that the work continue. At the time I thought that perhaps not everyone in the room quite grasped the seriousness of the situation, and how much work needed to be done to refine our plans. In retrospect, though, I think there might have been another explanation – that it was the Department of Finance that was seeking to set the pace, rather than their own bosses in the Central Bank and Financial Regulator. If so, this was a passing phase. Cooperation between institutions was generally quite good in the following months, and there was certainly no reluctance on the part of senior staff in the CBFSAI to give of their time and energy in the crisis.

As it turned out, planning continued for days and weeks on end, but the focus for that and the following weekend was heavily on Irish Nationwide as the most immediate problem.

In normal times, INBS should not have been a big problem to solve. We understood that, informally, the two biggest banks operating in the Irish market, AIB Bank and Bank of Ireland, had been approached months earlier by the Governor of the Central Bank. As we understood the situation, he had discussed in general terms the tightening liquidity situation, the problems in other jurisdictions and the necessity to be prepared for all eventualities. He wanted to be reassured that in the event of a problem the two larger banks would play a self-interested role in sorting out the problem. And the banks had, apparently, indicated a general willingness to be helpful. If a larger bank, say, Anglo-Irish Bank (Anglo), was in difficulty, this might be too big for them to handle, but the takeover of a smaller player by one or other of the two largest banks should be manageable.

So in the course of our discussions I told the Financial Regulator's senior staff that I thought the two big banks had to be called in and told that their time had come. The regulatory staff seemed a bit reluctant – were we really at that stage? But I stressed that we had always anticipated such a step if a smaller institution had a problem, and that was clearly the case now. To maintain the proper institutional order, and to avoid any indication that the public purse was freely available to solve a banking problem, I sat in a side room (presumably with others, I don't remember now), while the regulators met the two banks. The regulators received a strong refusal: the banks were concerned that INBS' very high property exposure would be too difficult for them to digest.

Here was a warning sign. Bank of Ireland, we were told, had taken a look at the INBS property loans many months before when INBS was looking for a buyer to take it over. Did their reluctance now in supporting INBS suggest we needed to get more and better data on the INBS property book for ourselves? But more than that, were the banks now more worried about their own vulnerability than we had expected? Certainly INBS had a proportionately larger commercial property book than most of the other institutions, but still the larger banks themselves had a huge property exposure.

There was a solution – or at least a partial one – to the data problem in INBS. Goldman Sachs had already been engaged by INBS to examine some of their lending for another purpose altogether. They had the staff and expertise, and they were willing to change their focus and instead to work to answer the Regulator's questions. They very quickly produced an assessment, based of course on information from INBS and its executives, as well as from documentary review, of the scale of difficulties with the INBS loan book. They described the property lending, the very high level of bespoke structures, the unexpected amount of equity participation, the sizeable exposure to particular parts of the London market and, somewhat worryingly, the extent to which most of these business relationships relied on only the personal expertise and knowledge of a small number of people. Protecting value in the loan book might therefore be more than usually dependent on keeping and maintaining the focus of the executives concerned. But otherwise the assessment was perhaps a bit more upbeat than we had feared at the time, and in retrospect and with the benefit of hindsight was hopelessly optimistic. On Sunday 21 September 2008, I heard their assessment in a meeting with Basil Geoghegan from Goldman Sachs and various others. While it might be difficult to get 100 per cent back on some of the loans they had issued, there was nothing to suggest any losses could not be absorbed by INBS' own capital. In other words, they seemed to be in some trouble, would need some help, but were probably solvent.

Goldman Sachs' assessment would take some short time to complete, but work on the potential rescue of INBS continued. So by the end of the weekend of 13–14 September there was an outline plan for an intervention in Irish Nationwide Building Society (which could of course apply with whatever modifications might be required to other institutions as necessary). The plan, which was never finalised because the situation kept changing, provided for the institution to be taken into state 'protection' – in other words, nationalised. If it became clear that the institution's ongoing liquidity drain was not going to be staunched, meetings would be called over a weekend, a new chairman and some new directors would be selected and formal directions from the regulator would be drafted so that the existing management would, in effect, be under instructions from the regulator to be cooperative for the few short days it was envisaged it would take to bring a Nationalisation Bill to the Oireachtas and have it passed. Lists were made of all the individuals and institutions who would have to be contacted to ensure that all of this could happen. Regulators in other jurisdictions would have to be informed, the ECB would have to be consulted, and arrangements for communications with depositors and shareholders would be put in place to reassure them.

The civil service head of information technology and the Department of Finance press officer were told to make contingency arrangements to have a new call centre up and running on very short notice – to cope with the potential for thousands of concerned calls from members of the public – and messages of the type that would be needed for press and public were drafted. In such an event, bank branch managers would be contacted over the weekend to allow them to be informed of developments before opening on Monday.

At all costs, the terrible demonstration effect of allowing queues of depositors to develop outside branches – a very public 'run' on the bank – was to be avoided.[1] Branch managers in INBS were already experiencing queueing at their branches – if a queue was developing just ahead of opening time, they might open a few minutes early, or if the branch was busy, they would ensure that the queue would snake inside the office rather than pass the front door. This was not entirely academic. At one stage in September 2008 I heard from a bank that a camera crew had burst into one of its branches demanding to know where the queue had gone. They had been misinformed that depositors were lining up to withdraw funds.

Of course, the public were aware of possible problems in the banks. They were discussed regularly in the media, and there had been scarcely a month in the recent past when some major bank or other did not get into difficulty. There was a lot of speculation as a result of the US sub-prime crisis, the Northern Rock events around the same time – in which a bank with an Irish office was saved only by a guarantee (later leading to nationalisation) by the UK Government – and the bailout of the Sachsen Landesbank, a publicly owned German bank with a subsidiary in Dublin's International Financial Services Centre. These events and more had marked the second half of 2007. And difficulties had continued in the US in 2008, with the collapse and takeover of Bear Sterns in March, Countrywide in trouble in May, and with new crises emerging in July, August and early September in the big US mortgage institutions.

In Europe, too, there had been some very public signs of problems. In April, the Bank of England had opened a special new liquidity arrangement, indicating the cash pressure most banks were feeling. The ECB was less expansive, but it too was producing increasing amounts of liquidity for the banking system, and developing new instruments for doing so.

Then, on 15 September 2008, Lehman Brothers, a New York-based bank, filed for bankruptcy. It was like an earthquake hit the financial system – no Government rescue, let the market work it out! Well the market was not well prepared for this event, and the ability of banks around the developed world to raise funds on money markets, especially ones like the US commercial paper market, simply dived. A gradually tightening liquidity noose constricting the financial sector's room to breathe, while not yet fatal, was given a sudden sharp yank.[2]

And of course the public in Ireland, as elsewhere, noticed, and they were worried. And then the public broadcaster, RTÉ, decided to get involved. George Lee, one of RTÉ's economic and business journalists, was filmed outside the old Dublin branch office of Northern Rock[3] asking whether the queues of depositors (cue file footage from the previous year) that had been seen outside that office would now be repeated at Irish banks. Joe Duffy's *Liveline* programme on Radio 1 entertained the worst fears of small depositors, without – it seemed – much attempt at reassurance. Fragile confidence appeared in danger of shattering. Regular technical email messages from INBS to the Central Bank, updating on their liquidity flows, contained more personal messages about counter staff in tears after dealing with customers terrified by the RTÉ coverage. Brian Lenihan told me afterwards that he had picked up the phone to ring the head of RTÉ to ask that they avoid creating a panic.

Of course, the underlying truth was that there were big and unavoidable problems in the Irish banking system – RTÉ was not wrong about that – and it was clear that the general public would not be reassured just by soothing official words, however many there were. Some action was required. A proposal was prepared for an increase in the level of protection on bank deposits. This protection had applied to the first €30,000 – in line with many European countries but well below the UK – and now it was to increase to €100,000, a level that would protect the deposits of most members of the public, numerically, but which would not of course protect the majority of bank deposits by value. In other words, most people would be protected because most people did not have large bank deposits.

But the majority of the money, being in large corporate and interbank deposits, would not be protected.

The decision was taken by the Government on a bright Saturday morning, 20 September 2008. There was not a regular meeting that day, so the consultation was done 'incorporeally'. The Secretary General to the Government, Dermot McCarthy, took a seat at one of the six or seven desks in the outer office of the Minister for Finance, where the many representations, notes and submissions, correspondence and phone calls received by the Minister are managed and co-ordinated, and he telephoned each Government Minister in turn, explaining the proposal and confirming their consent or otherwise. Cabinet confidentiality applies to these meetings, even when done in this manner, so I don't know what was said by any of the Ministers. But when Dermot confirmed that the Government was in agreement, we were able to inform the Minister's press office – just across the corridor, in a crowded, functional room facing on to Merrion Street – that they could go ahead with work on finalising and issuing the press release.

The measure did work well, as far as assuaging the concerns of the individual depositors, and the pressure on small deposits eased greatly. Irish Nationwide, most of whose deposits came from the smaller depositor, did not later have the same kind of liquidity pressures that were to be felt by the larger banks. Public panic was averted.

But it was no panacea. In fact, this extended deposit protection was almost worthless to the bigger depositors whose sentiment towards Irish banks could change overnight. No one involved expected anything other than a moment's respite, perhaps a little time to continue working and planning.

Well before that weekend, however, thoughts had turned to other institutions. If rapidly changing circumstances were such that the INBS loan book was becoming so much more troublesome, we had to have better and more up to date information on the other banks. We could use Goldman Sachs, up to a point, but there were reasons why they were not suitable to produce a broad-ranging assessment. It was, however, clear that a high-powered corporate finance house was going to be needed.

Unfortunately, there was a shortage of good teams available who were not already attached to existing banking organisations or without major conflicts of interest.

By the week ending 20 September, Morgan Stanley had been hovering in the background for a few days. I had received polite phone calls to give me their views on the current market situation and to reassure me that if ever we had need of them to do some work for us, they could be called on at short notice. So we called them.

And for about two days they did some excellent work for us – a very strong analysis based on publicly available information (they were not yet on contract and therefore not getting confidential data) of the Irish Life and Permanent's position. We had quickly raised our eyes from the immediate INBS problems to the growing problems of the other institutions. Unlike the other banks, Irish Life and Permanent (ILP), a banking and life assurance group whose banking arm was called Permanent TSB (PTSB), had limited commercial property exposures, but it had a very large mortgage book, heavily funded by shorter-term borrowings from the wholesale funding market. If that source were to dry up, ILP would become Ireland's Northern Rock.

We also, of course, had to build Anglo and even the two larger banks into our thinking. We needed Morgan Stanley to quickly engage with the situation of all the banks – and then they dropped out. They decided that they had too big a conflict of interest arising from past work – and hoped-for future work – with Anglo and other institutions. I was annoyed. These were the guys who had come to us looking for business and they were letting us down even before they started. That being the case, there was no point trying to hold on to them and the search for the right advisers had to restart.

Meanwhile, we continued to work with the NTMA as the Minister's expert advisers, and with the Central Bank and Financial Regulator's staff, to further prepare for whatever was to happen next. The situation was complex, and the environment continued to get worse. Lehman's was not the only casualty. Merrill Lynch had to be taken over by Bank of America and the giant insurer, AIG, had to go to the US authorities seeking short-term financing. An update on 17 September 2008 to the Minister for Finance noted that the Irish stock exchange had lost about half of its value since the early part of 2007, that the main Irish bank stocks had each lost more than 70 per cent of their value since their peak, and that AIB and Anglo had lost 15 per cent and 20 per cent respectively in just two days. Worse, perhaps, was that the cost of insuring against loss in Irish bank debt had risen 30 per cent or more in just a few days, which meant that some people in the market were losing faith in the certainty of being repaid on Irish bank debt. The note finished with an understatement: 'international difficulties are therefore amplifying pressures in the domestic banking system'.

Officials were meeting regularly. In the Department of Finance work was continuing with staff in the Attorney General's office on legislation to nationalise a bank or building society, but also to allow for other supports for the banking system, including guarantees, but we felt that guarantees could never be a whole solution. The Central Bank was monitoring liquidity of the banks very carefully. The NTMA was working with us to identify approaches to dealing with failing banks, and along with us were pressing the Central Bank and Regulator to deepen our understanding of the banks' loan books.

During the second half of that month a particular pattern developed of organising meetings to move policy along and to finalise proposals to be recommended to the Minister or Government, and this continued for some months after. Typically, the technical work which had been going on over the previous few days via emails, phone calls, meetings in Dame Street or Merrion Street or at the NTMA offices on Grand Canal Street, would culminate in a sort of 'Jumbo' meeting in which the most senior people of the public institutions concerned would have a focussed discussion based on the information and conclusions of the technical work which had been going on. Often, these meetings would be preceded by a big technical meeting (in many cases chaired by myself) in which all of the current information and technical discussions could be discussed and summarised in preparation for the higher level meeting to follow. In these high level meetings, I often organised the sequence of the discussion, but everyone had their chance to speak and the senior staff present then came to a conclusion. There was one such high level meeting on 18 September, for example, when the Minister for Finance, the Governor of the Central Bank, the Chief Executive of the NTMA, the Chairman of the Financial Regulator and various others met, and it was decided to propose the increase in the deposit guarantee limits described above, as well as to draft a statement for the Minister to use in calming tensions in the markets. Often these meetings led to a requirement for immediate action, so some of the people present might be despatched to draft a statement or to organise further technical work while the meeting continued.

But the circle of people involved was, necessarily, widening. Confidentiality was very important, but no one was pretending that there was no critical work going on – it would have been impossible to do so. Even some weeks before, one diligent official who often worked very late told me that he had noticed that some of the people working in the banking area seemed to be present in the office at extraordinary hours, and that he understood what that must mean – he promised total discretion. One colleague on the banking team had explained his absence from family events by saying that he was working on the budget, which was to be earlier than normal that year. It was his pre-teen daughter who noted that this was strange as he had not worked on the budget before. For months we had done our work in secret, with only a very small team of people, afraid that preparation for difficulties in the banking system would be interpreted in public as an expectation of them and lead to a bank run. It was a relief to have some further support, and with all that was happening around the world there was no longer any reason to hide that we were working on the banking system, though there were still many details which were highly confidential.

The widening circle of those involved now included Arthur Cox solicitors, brought in on the recommendation of the Attorney General, and Merrill Lynch, brought in on a €7 million contract by the NTMA. After the 'loss' of Morgan Stanley, Michael Somers of the NTMA very helpfully spoke to Bill McDonough, the Chairman of Merrill Lynch (Merrills), whom he apparently knew, and asked for a team of advisers from them to be headed by Henrietta Baldock. Henrietta was polite, calm and well-liked by her team, which included market and bank restructuring experts and which had very useful access to the wider resources of their group (notwithstanding that over

22

time they were to be absorbed into Bank of America). Having sourced the team, the NTMA then asked that the Minister to 'direct' them to contract Merrills to meet some legal nicety or other.

Later, many people noted that this was a big fee for what seemed like a few days' work. In fact, the team was contracted for a year. It was still a sizable fee, but these kinds of companies do command that kind of money. In the past I have known of cases where corporate finance advisers earning huge fees would go back to their clients to say that given how hard they had worked on a particular project, they actually think they should be paid more. The size of the fees gave us pause for thought, but only for a moment. In truth, this was a small cost relative to the size of the problem, however strange a world it was that led to mid-level staff, however highly skilled, being hired out at over a million apiece.

Even at this late stage, in the ten days before the bank guarantee, it was difficult to say what shape the looming crisis would take. For sure, we had to accept there would be some bank failures, in the sense that banks could not function properly without some outside help. INBS was in effect already failed, if apparently not insolvent, but INBS was not the most pressing problem. The deposit outflows were reducing in the days following the increase in the threshold for the deposit guarantee scheme, and the sense of immediate crisis in that quarter had thus eased a touch. ILP and Anglo, however, were both losing funding at the wholesale level, as were the two bigger banks, AIB and Bank of Ireland. There was a difference, albeit, that affected, at the very least, the pace at which these institutions might get into difficulty.

Basically, at the end of every day, a bank has either a surplus or a deficit of liquidity. That means that either they have more funds than they need to meet that day's liabilities, in which case they have to find a home for those funds, or they are short of liquid funds for that day, in which case they have to find someone to lend them the difference between what they have and what they need. This is not unusual; it is normal banking business and the amounts are generally fairly small relative to the size of the bank concerned. And the solution is quite simple too – if you have excess funding, you make a deposit with the Central Bank, which will probably pay you less interest than you would have hoped to get on the market – and if you have a shortage of liquid funds, you ask the Central Bank to lend you what you need for the day. Again, this is normal.

When the central bank lends to your bank, it does so happily, because it takes collateral for its loan. It knows if your bank did not pay back the short-term loan, the collateral would cover the loss, with a bit left over. So normal is this operation that central banks maintain lists of 'eligible collateral'. In other words, they have a list of assets they will accept as collateral, and those they will not. Generally government bonds are acceptable on the spot, so are other types of easily traded bonds or securities, maybe some types of inter-institutional loans. But they don't want individual mortgages as collateral, for example – they are too hard to price and not easily traded. And they don't want big one-of-a-kind commercial loans, again because they too are not readily tradable and priced.

As liquidity pressures on the banking systems increased, more and more of them – not just in Ireland but very widely in Europe and the US – were relying increasingly on central bank loans to make up the difference in their liquid funds. But ILP's main assets were those individual mortgages, and Anglo had a lot of big one-off commercial loans. They were rapidly running out of the type of assets that they could use to get funds from the Central Bank – and the Irish Central Bank had to follow Eurosystem rules in deciding what collateral was required. A continuation of the difficulties that they were having in getting funds from the public or from other banks would push them to the point where they needed more funds from the Central Bank than the Central Bank could legally lend to them under the normal rules. AIB and Bank of Ireland were much better provided for in terms of eligible collateral.

Worse, for different reasons, Anglo and ILP fell into just the types of bank which lenders had quite recently loved to lend to, but now wished not to do so. Increasingly, all of the banks were finding that lenders they had previously relied on would give them less money, or none, or would lend only for increasingly short periods of time – overnight, or for a week for example, instead of for a month or more.

Whatever the longer-term solvency of the institutions – and this will be discussed further later – they clearly were moving towards a liquidity cliff. The moment they could not get funds, whether from the Central Bank or elsewhere, to meet all their liabilities on any given day, there would be a major crisis. One could hope that conditions might improve, but there was no immediate let up, especially after Lehmans.

It is hard to describe now the atmosphere at the time. Work was very intensive – late nights and seven days a week. The sense of pressure was also intense, and a big part of my job was keeping all the teams – not just in the Department of Finance but also in Dame Street and Treasury Buildings – on an even keel, working together. I was working most closely with William Beausang and his team in the Department of Finance, with Pat Neary and Con Horan in the Financial Regulator, Tony Grimes and Brian Halpin in the Central Banking arm of the Dame Street system, Henrietta and her team from

Merrills, and of course with my own bosses, David Doyle, as Secretary General of the Department of Finance, and Brian Lenihan, the Minister. In the NTMA, Brendan McDonagh and John Corrigan were my speed dials, and they were briefing their CEO, Michael Somers, on a daily basis. For a part of this time John Hurley was missing while recovering from serious medical treatment. It was a relief when he came back (judging by his appearance, it must have been against doctors' orders, because he was obviously not well), because the Dame Street system clearly worked better when there was a single person to co-ordinate. Michael Somers was present for most of September, but went to New York, with John Corrigan, for an investor conference at the end of September, and thus was not physically present on the night of 29 September when the Government's guarantee decision was made.

Sometimes the stress of the situation would manifest itself in an angry word, or an expression of frustration, but mostly there was not enough time for that – we had to keep moving forward. Although the total number of people involved was relatively small, meetings tended to be crowded affairs, often on short notice, sometimes with some people ringing in from outside to a phone switched to loudspeaker mode in the room.

Both David Doyle and I were speaking to Minister Lenihan every day, sometimes for a moment or two but often in long, drawn out discussions of the situation and the options, which were limited. At times the Minister would say in apparent frustration, 'but Kevin' or 'but David', 'this is very serious', more to himself than to us, I think because we were hardly unaware of the seriousness of the situation. We provided him with regular updates and our understanding was that he was in close touch with the Taoiseach at all times. The Minister was also, of course, speaking to many other people, and the broadcaster David McWilliams has written about one such encounter.[4] The Minister volunteered to me later that this account was inaccurate on one or two points – in particular denying some negative comment in relation to the Department of Finance – but the truth was that McWilliams' account was basically correct. The Minister was interested in hearing the comments of persons outside his official advisers (particularly important for a new Minister, perhaps), and there was no obligation for him to tell his civil servants about these discussions.

Throughout the build up to these crisis weeks we had provided the Minister with briefing points that he could use at Government meetings, if required. But it was strictly up to him to decide how much of the briefing to use. During his time as Minister for Finance he was concerned that sensitive information could not be trusted to the whole cabinet because – in his view – at least one of his colleagues would not treat the information received with discretion. This had consequences later.

The point is that there were a lot of people available to advise, but absent a major improvement in market conditions or some international initiative, there was no 'good' option. If things continued as they had been, the Irish people were going to suffer. Simple as that.

On the evening of 24 September 2008, a further meeting was held to consider the options that were available. Preceded by a meeting of the various technical groups, there were about 15 people in a conference room in Merrion Street, and the atmosphere was tense. In attendance were the Taoiseach and the Secretary General to the Government, the Attorney General, the Central Bank governor and his Director General, Tony Grimes, Pat Neary and Jim Farrell, CEO and Chair of the Financial Regulator, respectively, and of course the Minister for Finance, with my immediate boss, David Doyle and myself.

Michael Somers and John Corrigan attended from the NTMA.
From the various advisory groups, Merrill Lynch, Goldman
Sachs (briefly), Arthur Cox and PWC were represented, the
latter having at last been commissioned by the Financial Regulator to do more in-depth analysis on the funding and loan
books of the banks.[5] Various possibilities for intervention in
the banking system were considered, including lending to
the banks to help their funding position, providing them with
government bonds which they could use to access Central
Bank funding and giving them guarantees to allow them to
access funds from the public and on the money markets. The
nationalisation of one or more banks was also very much on
the agenda. I made clear that the situation was urgent – probably stating the obvious. The discussion also made clear that
there was a lot of uncertainty about the underlying future of
the banks. The Financial Regulator remained of the view that
there was no evidence of insolvency, for example at Anglo
Irish bank, but of course that situation could change. It was
agreed that further work would be done to examine the various intervention mechanisms being considered, and on en-
abling legislation.

That work continued into the night and the next few days.
Emails whizzed around the ether, at various levels of the official bodies and advisors engaged in this effort. David Doyle
asked the NTMA to prepare an assessment of the impact of
guarantees to banks on the State's own creditworthiness. They
suggested that at a minimum there would be a significant increase in the State's borrowing costs and some damage to our
credit rating. The external environment was not helping – in
the US, Washington Mutual was the latest bank to get into
difficulties. By US standards it was relatively small, but still
much larger than any of the Irish institutions, and the manner

in which it was resolved (without protections for bondholders and some depositors) was regretted later by many commentators, who felt it should have been treated as 'too big to fail'.

In Europe there were problems too. Ireland's representative at the EFC (the Economic and Financial Committee at which senior officials from Finance Ministries, as well as representatives of the ECB and EC, met to discuss important developments) relayed back that there was a lot of 'coded talk', but that it seemed there was an expectation of the failure of a large European Bank over the weekend.

There was a meeting of the Central Bank Board on the 25th so some of the Dame Street people were not in attendance with the Minister for Finance that day, but they were represented, and Oliver Whelan and Brendan McDonagh from the NTMA were also on hand. The services of Arthur Cox were becoming indispensable, and they were present too. Work continued again on the following day, as discussions began to centre around a set of options put together into a presentation by Merrill Lynch (by now joined by Henrietta Baldock's boss, Andrea Orcelli). The meetings on the 26th finished with instructions for further work and my notes indicated this group was to gather again at the NTMA offices in Treasury Buildings on Sunday, 28 September. The set of options, together with pros and cons, included the possibility of providing broad guarantees for all the main banks, but also noted that there were downsides with this approach.

The idea of a broad guarantee – in effect a Government promise in relation to a broad spectrum of the banking system, and in relation to a broad range of their deposits and borrowings, that the Government would ensure that the depositors and lenders concerned would be protected from loss – was not a new idea. Some guarantees had been a part of many, perhaps most, bank crisis interventions in the past, and a broad guarantee had been a feature of, for example, the successful management of the Swedish bank crisis in the 1990s. We had been hearing on-and-off since March/April of that year of prominent people in the Irish financial scene who were advocating a broad Government promise of some sort as a mechanism to reassure the market and bank depositors that all would be well in the Irish banking system. Some of these people had contacted various officials, including John Hurley, the Governor of the Central Bank, with this proposition, but it was not part of official policy at any level. Moreover, in September there were further such suggestions as funds flowed out of the banks in Ireland. But I have no reason to think that this amounted to a co-ordinated lobbying exercise. I would be surprised, though, if at least some of the people involved were not talking to each other. It was not astonishing, then, when a proposal for a formal Government guarantee to the Irish banking system was advocated by economist David McWilliams in his newspaper column that weekend.[6]

But when the official parties met on 25 and 26 September 2008, the broad guarantee was one of a number of options for action being considered. In retrospect – because it was the option eventually chosen by Government – it takes on much more prominence, but at those technical meetings it was not emerging as the most favoured approach of the people in those rooms. Still, the broad guarantee was something that had to be considered along with other possible interventions.

The three days between the meetings on Friday 26 and the meeting on the night of 29 September and early morning of 30 September at which the bank guarantee was discussed, and then recommended to the Government, in retrospect seems like a long time. Legal teams, officials, advisors all fitted a lot of work into that small space of time. The legislation in preparation had to be refined and adjusted, further study was required on the European State aid rules – about which more later – advisors and central bankers queried the developing liquidity position of the banks, so plenty to be done. But in fact, there were also new considerations to be addressed.

Over that weekend it became clear that Hypo Real Estate (HRE), a big German bank, was running into trouble. In the UK, there were signals that Bradford and Bingley, a former building society which had demutualised, was in trouble – it announced big job losses on 25 September and its nationalisation was announced on the following Monday, 29 September. The Americans were still under huge pressure, and had themselves announced a big rescue plan, known as TARP, which was clearly controversial, though at that stage was expected to pass through Congress.

The HRE problem was the more immediate one for us. A couple of years before, HRE had taken over a bank based in the Dublin docklands called DEPFA bank. DEPFA was on the face of it a relatively low risk operation. The bulk of its lending was to public sector entities and it raised money in part using relatively safe 'pfandbrief' instruments, or asset-covered securities, as they were called in Ireland. But they were also accessing a lot of funds on a short-term basis through wholesale money markets – the same money markets that had been increasingly reluctant to lend to banks, even before the Lehman Brothers shock, and then got a lot worse. So now DEPFA was in need of help, which was a big complication for its parent HRE.

The question then was whether Ireland was willing to expend any resources to help DEPFA, for example by providing guarantees to its lenders. At this juncture my recollection is a bit uncertain, but I do recall that we – Ireland – did get asked that question in the form of a query to the Central Bank Governor, John Hurley, from the German Bundesbank. Would Ireland want to participate in a big German effort to save HRE? John said that he thought this unlikely: DEPFA was a big enough bank in asset terms, but its assets and its liabilities mostly lay abroad. It could not be regarded as having 'systemic importance' for the Irish banking system or economy. Besides, we needed to hold our firepower for the increasingly immediate threat to the domestic banking system.

I think it was about a week later that I received a telephone call from DEPFA staff very late in the evening. The first rescue interventions for their parent company, HRE, had not been sufficient and DEPFA executives had been told that they would be closing their doors the next day and allowed to go bankrupt – in effect, Lehman-like – and that hundreds would be out of employment immediately. They needed to know if there was any possibility of support from the Irish Government. I knew the answer, but I promised to double-check my understanding of the situation, and rang them back some time later with confirmation of the bad news. No support available. In fact, the German decision was not so dramatic in the end – DEPFA was not immediately closed up – but I felt heartbroken for those people trying in the middle of the night to save their livelihoods. Unfortunately, there would be many in worse circumstances in the following months.

The planned meeting at Treasury Buildings took place on Sunday 28 September to further outline and refine the list of options for intervention that the Government might consider. Separately, there was an informal meeting that afternoon in Dame Street. The Central Bank premises there dominate the skyline, and the building is designed so that the corridors on most floors run around the outside of the building, so a person who walks the length of the corridor will get a wonderful 360 degree panorama of the whole of Dublin. I always looked north, to the big red brick church which marked the parish where I grew up, and most Dubliners could see the landmarks of their home districts from the Central Bank tower. The layout was a bit different on the seventh floor, where the most senior staff had offices. There was a gathering there in the Governor's office to talk informally over the current position. Brian Lenihan was present, as was I, along with the Governor, Hurley, and some of his senior colleagues.

We had been called together at short notice and I think the intention was simply for the Governor and Minister to exchange views on the current situation. In that regard, DEPFA was a complication which was discussed, but the more important topic was the liquidity of the banks. Anglo was close to zero in terms of available cash: a few more days at the current run rate was all they could expect, and we had to be prepared for the contingency that they might not even have that. On balance, though, the Central Bank thought they could last a week before running out of funds to meet day-to-day obligations, which would mean that big decisions would be needed the following weekend at the latest. Others were also very tight on liquidity, but Anglo's position was the worst. John Hurley looked terrible that day, still suffering from his recent illness. Brian Lenihan's own very serious illness was yet to surface. I was looking out the giant panes of glass in the Governor's office. Huge clouds were gathering and darkening in the twilight over the River Liffey, and I thought how a superstitious person might think them quite ominous.

The next day, Monday, 29 September 2008, was interesting in all the wrong ways. But it started as a mere continuation of the events of the previous week. Both PWC and Merrill Lynch had information to give us that underpinned the rather obvious conclusion that things were perched on a knife edge.

PWC staff engaged by the Financial Regulator had been hard at work analysing the funding position of the three worst case banks going into the new week. All had been losing deposits, so the funding position was weakening, but we knew that. Ironically, Irish Nationwide, where our troubles had started, was not in the worst position. It had lost a lot of customer deposits in the three weeks that had passed since 8 September, but they had a lot of cash, and since the increase in the deposit guarantee limits for small depositors their rate of loss had eased considerably. They were due to make big payments on medium-term borrowings which would mature in December, but even with a steady loss of deposits they would not be in immediate cash flow difficulties.

ILP was in a much worse position. If they had a very bad week, they could be out of cash in a matter of days, with no assets suitable to use as collateral for central bank borrowings. They had some hopes of producing collateralisable assets[7] in the coming weeks, however, if they could last until then.

Even worse was Anglo. They might be able to manage a small positive balance at the end of the week, but there were real concerns that things could get much worse. First, even if things went relatively well, there were big deposits due to be repaid on Tuesday, 30 September, which could create a small shortfall in their cash position that day (remembering that we are talking about a world where 'small' is measured in hundreds of millions of euros).

Second, the benign scenario was contingent on being able to package certain commercial mortgages into a type of security that they could use as collateral to obtain central bank loans, called a commercial mortgage-backed security, or CMBS. This was due to happen mid-week, and while this kind of thing is relatively routine for banks, it is not usually done with such limited room for manoeuvre in terms of time, and with such potentially dire consequences if the deadline was missed. Theoretically, if they were a day late Anglo could have a position that would see them cash positive, if only just, at the end of the week, but to no avail, because without any cash they would have had to close their doors mid-week. Obviously, they would be hoping for official help, if this sort of scenario arose.

But that was the benign scenario. Their own worst case scenario was much worse, here described by PWC in an email sent that day:

> … under management's "worst case" scenarion the shortfall increases to E2,449m on 3 October. If the CMBS is not completed this increases to E4.6 billion. To avoid this the withdrawal of deposits needs to cease, assuming that the interbank and capital markets remain effectively closed for the immediate future (sic).

Clearly, deposit and interbank flows that Monday would tell a lot about the future of the Irish banking system.

September 29 turned out to be quite a day. Banks were falling over and having to be supported by Governments across the US and Europe. In the morning it was announced that HRE would be supported by a consortium of German lenders by arrangement with the German authorities. In the US, Wachovia Bank was in need of support with information that it was likely to be taken over. In the UK, the Bradford and Bingley Building Society was to be nationalised, as already noted. The night before, the Belgian, Dutch and Luxembourg governments had announced an €11 billion bailout of Fortis Bank, which only a year or so before was being trumpeted as the model of a new style of European bank, truly international – now evidenced by the international nature of its bailout.

There was trouble too for the Franco-Belgian bank Dexia, whose shares were collapsing, and Belgian authorities were making protective statements. In fact, it also required a bailout not too many hours later. Dexia had lost money on US sub-prime investments, it appeared, and on Lehmans, and while the French Government appeared to be distancing itself from a potential rescue of Dexia, which it said was a Belgian concern, the market was aware of its position as a lender to a large number of French local authorities. In Iceland, there was a rescue for Glitnir bank, their third biggest lender.

In the midst of all this, there was no reason to expect a good day in Ireland, and it was clear early on that the Irish banks' shares were going to take a hammering that day, reflecting their weak position and the desperate situation in Europe.

In a rough first draft I made that day of speaking points for possible use by Minister Brian Lenihan, the international position was summed up as follows:

> However, the international situation has been getting increasingly bad, and in three weeks there have been at least twelve major financial institutions filing for bankruptcy, rescued by the State or acquired by rivals while under stress, culminating this weekend in the situations at Fortis and HypoBank[8] – the latter having a very large (in asset terms) Irish subsidiary. Interbank, commercial paper and corporate deposit markets have been drying up or funds have been available (sic). As a result, the Irish financial sector is under extreme pressure.

That afternoon there was more news to worry about. Matt Pass, one of the Merrill Lynch team, informed us that Standard and Poor's, an important credit rating agency, was likely to issue a statement downgrading the credit rating of the main Irish banks. In effect, they were in a vicious cycle: their inability to raise funds made them less creditworthy, which in turn made fundraising more difficult, and the credit rating downgrade would accelerate the downward cycle.

By close of business that day, it would be clear that Anglo could not sustain the pressure on its funding position. They had lost deposits, they were just about out of cash, had no more collateral available to allow them to borrow from the normal central bank facilities, the next day they could expect to be another €2 billion or so in the red, perhaps €8 or €10 billion within a short few days, and trapped in a downward cycle with no exit.

So, of course, there had to be a discussion that evening.

2

The Night of the Guarantee

The Taoiseach's office sits at the very end of a long L-shaped corridor in Government Buildings. It is separate from but part of the same complex as the Department of Finance building and the Attorney General's office, the latter two fronting the street. To get to the Taoiseach's office from the Department of Finance, one can walk down Dublin's Merrion Street and in the front gate to the courtyard, at the back of which is the Department of the Taoiseach building, or one can go down through the basement and emerge into the courtyard through a side alley, avoiding the street altogether. In either case, one must pass the usually friendly service officer at the main door of the Taoiseach's building and walk up one floor. Then, turning southwards, one reaches the left turn that leads to the Taoiseach's office, accessible through an outer office where his private secretary and colleagues manage the flow of people and documents that are the stuff of much of his day to day work.

As corridors of power go, these are nice but not lavish. The corridor is wide and there are well appointed, though not magnificent, offices and conference rooms along the right hand side of the corridor, while on the left, there is a view over the courtyard of the complex and the fountain in the middle. At the very end of the corridor is a small meeting room, and to the right of the corridor, directly opposite the Taoiseach's outer office, a smaller waiting room. Taoisigh are busy people, so any visit to the Taoiseach might entail passing some time in this rather sterile and somewhat pokey waiting room.

I still don't know who called the meeting, but it was inevitable that there would be one that evening, given the events of the day. My boss, David Doyle, told me to be over at the Taoiseach's office by 6.00 p.m. Representatives from the Central Bank, Financial Regulator, Arthur Cox and others were in attendance at various points in the evening. Officials from the NTMA arrived a bit later, at my request. Some of the Taoiseach's own advisors were there too – Joe Lennon and Peter Clinch. William Beausang was there from the Department of Finance, and he told me that he had our small crisis team on standby across the courtyard to do whatever might be necessary. At some point I became aware that the heads of the two biggest banks were to be in attendance in the building some time later, though I never had the understanding that the meeting was called at their request, as has been suggested over the years in some media outlets. Rather, as I understand it, it was the case that the two banks jointly decided to ask to meet the Taoiseach, and that this request coincided with the separate arrangements for a meeting between the official bodies concerned.

There seemed to be a few disorganised minutes while people arrived, passing on bits of the latest information in hushed voices around the waiting room or in the corridor just outside, but soon things sorted themselves out. There was to be a group of senior officials to meet the Taoiseach, Brian Cowen, and others were to remain outside in support. I was anxious to be in the room with the Taoiseach – albeit just about the most 'junior' person for a good deal of the time – because it was important that someone be there who had participated in many of the working meetings over the past few days.

David Doyle and Minister Brian Lenihan were there. Jim Farrell and Pat Neary from the Regulator and John Hurley and Tony Grimes from the Central Bank represented the Dame Street system. The Attorney General, Paul Gallagher, and a solicitor from Arthur Cox, Eugene McCague, were also in the room later. And of course the Taoiseach attended himself. William Beausang was in attendance at the outset, but not later on. These people and some others came in and out as required, and indeed I was not present for every moment of the meeting either as I would occasionally have to step out on some errand or other.

I was of course nervous – I imagine everyone there was – but I was also somewhat relieved. At last, there was no more room for wait-and-see. The Taoiseach had called a meeting to make big decisions, his stature would count with the other players and we would get some direction for action. I was confident that my team, with the Attorney General's staff of lawyers and parliamentary drafters, could deliver any legislation required very quickly, as we already had prepared draft legislation which could allow for guarantees, special liquidity swap arrangements, nationalisation (bank or building society – the technicalities differed but the principles were much the same), direct loans and so forth. Thanks to our various meetings and brainstorming sessions, some of which the Minister and Taoiseach had been involved in, we had a range of options to describe, with pros and cons for each.

Moreover, if there was a need to apply Government money directly, the authorities had a 'fighting fund' of sorts arranged, so that taking cash and fungible securities together, as well as some limited scope to apply the Central Bank balance sheet,

we could have many billions of euro ready at very short notice, perhaps as much as €20 billion.

The meeting – perhaps in truth best described as a rolling
series of meetings – that took place that evening was business-
like and professional. I have seen the then Taoiseach impatient
and frustrated at times, but at this moment he was calm and in
charge, and his calmness helped to ease tension and allow the
business to move along.

But he did surprise me quite early on. I had expected that
we would discuss guarantees for banks among the options for
consideration – indeed, by then I thought that some guarantees
were inevitable. But the Taoiseach raised the issue of a broad
pre-emptive guarantee early in the discussion. It seemed to
me that he already had a preference for this approach going
into the meeting, or at least that it was the baseline approach
against which every other option would be considered. Brian
Cowen has since made clear that he had not made up his mind
as the meeting started,[9] but it was certainly my impression at
the time that his mind was formed quite early in the evening.

This was not the preferred approach of our advisers in Merrill Lynch, I was sure, and I stepped out of the room to send a
quick email message to Merrill: 'in meet with taoiseach – need
note on pros and cons of guarantee a sap' (sic). Towards the
early part of the evening I also made a few phone calls to find
Brendan McDonagh from NTMA and ask him to come into
Government buildings. I valued his advice and support and
wanted him close by.

Of course, I already knew the pros and cons of the guarantee option, in outline at least, as they were listed out in a document prepared the previous Friday, but I felt it was important
that the meeting would have confirmation of Merrill's position. Moreover, events had moved on quite a bit in the previ-

ous 24 hours, so the balance of advantage might have changed somewhat in even that short period, and I wanted to be certain that I understood the position clearly.

There was a lengthy discussion of the situation and the options, especially the guarantee option. Tony Grimes spoke about the funding position of the banks. John Hurley explained his understanding of the ECB and the European position. He noted that the ECB President, Jean-Claude Trichet, had stressed that it was essential for European and Irish financial stability that there be no bank failures in Europe. But, more worryingly, Trichet had also confirmed that there was no European initiative in the works which might ameliorate the situation. It was always possible that a number of larger countries would get together to design an initiative without consultation with relative minnows like Ireland, but it was most unlikely that Trichet would be out of the loop on any such initiative. The Irish central bankers were also clear that their own balance sheet was not large enough to make large loans to Irish banks outside the framework of the European System of Central Banks and the ECB. They had been very insistent on the need to have Government funds available to lend to banks.

The financial regulator spoke about the current solvency situation of the banks, maintaining the position that they were solvent, if not without difficulties.

It seems to me in retrospect that while the Department of Finance representatives, including the Minister, were more wary about the dangers of a broad bank guarantee, the Dame Street representatives (from the Central Bank and Financial Regulator) all strongly favoured the broad guarantee approach, on balance at least.

Minister Lenihan and I seemed to be the most concerned about possible downsides to this approach, but at some stage in the evening the Minister's views moved towards the consensus favouring the broad guarantee option. I heard the explanation of this a couple of years later. The Minister reminded me that the meeting had been suspended for a time so that he and the Taoiseach could have a private discussion. According to the Minister, during that private discussion they decided to present a united front around the broad guarantee option. But so far as I can recall, they did not actually announce that but rather let the meeting move toward that position.

There had been a Government meeting the previous day, Sunday the 28th, to discuss the forthcoming Budget – advanced from December to October to deal with the growing level of shortfall in the State's own financial position – and I have wondered to what extent this meeting might have influenced the Taoiseach's position. As Minister for Finance, Lenihan would be expected to be in a position to give an update to any Government meeting taking place around that time, and he had been provided with short speaking points in case that arose, but there was no discussion of the banking crisis on the agenda for that day, and Ministers had no way to know just then that there would be such a crucial meeting the following day. However, evidence given at the Oireachtas Banking Inquiry ('the Banking Inquiry') during the course of its hearings in 2015 by the Minister of the Environment at the time of the guarantee, John Gormley, suggests that there was some discussion of the broad guarantee approach on the margins of the Government meeting, and indeed that the David McWilliams article mentioned earlier was discussed,[10] and it had featured firmly also in the discussions the previous Thursday at the Central Bank Board. But it seems clear now that there was no Government decision on the matter, even informally, taken by that Sunday. The decision took place only after the discussion on the night and early morning of Monday the 29th and Tuesday the 30th.

While all of the initial discussions in the Taoiseach's office among the State agencies involved had been going on, Dermot Gleeson and Eugene Sheehy, the Chairman and Chief Executive of AIB, and Richard Burrows and Brian Goggin, Chairman and 'Governor' of Bank of Ireland, had arrived in the building and were waiting outside for some time – I presume they were in one of several conference rooms on the same floor. They were asked to join the meeting. They sat along one side of the table, the Taoiseach at the head of the table on their left, the Attorney General, Minister Lenihan, myself, David Doyle opposite them, others filling the rest of their side of the table and the table end opposite the Taoiseach.

I had met Sheehy and Goggin in the past: both seemed very substantial, serious individuals. Sheehy was friendly, Goggin seemed to me a bit more aloof, but courteous. I had never met Burrows, and my only previous direct encounter with Dermot Gleeson was in the formal setting of a commercial arbitration in which his client had sought millions in compensation for losses they claimed to have incurred on currency movements after the introduction of the euro. I had been a witness for the public body they had claimed against, and Gleeson had cross-examined me. It was a nil-all draw, I think. Gleeson, too, was an individual of some considerable stature, a former attorney general and regarded as one of Ireland's foremost barristers. But there was no reason to expect him to have a special insight into short-term money markets, and he let his CEO do much of the talking.

These bankers' message was stark. They knew well how vulnerable were the weaker banks, like Anglo, and were careful to distance themselves from the Anglo position. Sheehy described the market experience of that day. Both banks were finding it harder to attract funds. The willingness of market participants to make deposits or lend to Irish banks for longer periods, such as for one to three months, was greatly reduced, and the two banks were increasingly reliant on shorter-term funding – monies made available only for a day or a week. Soon, they would find themselves in breach of regulatory guidelines governing the average 'duration' of these types of deposits. Sheehy said that, for example, on one unsuccessful phone call seeking funds from an international bank, the AIB employee on the call had overheard a comment between two traders at the other end of the line: 'no quote for Ireland'. In other words, he argued, there would be no market differentiation between the Irish banks – all were being tarred with the same brush, and all would have funding problems. On their estimates, although both had substantial liquidity cushions, the circumstances were so extreme that even these two most substantial Irish banks might run out of funds in a matter of weeks. They wanted a guarantee from the Government in very broad terms, and they wanted insulation and differentiation from, in particular, Anglo, which they argued could only come from a nationalisation of that bank.

Taking these two banks at face value on their funding position, the situation now was that Anglo was already out of cash, ILP could be in a similar position by the end of the week and INBS was draining funds slowly but would eventually run out. The EBS building society had not yet been flashing the same warning signals, but would presumably also be infected. A worrying situation had become a desperate one in just a few short days.

With the passage of time I no longer remember precisely every aspect of the sequence of events on that night. The bankers came in, gave their views, exited, and then were invited back for further discussion. But (and despite some suggestions contradicting some aspects, which I have heard since), the following is clear to me:

- They outlined the market position, as I have noted above, and explicitly sought a very broad guarantee, providing suggested wording.

- They asked that Anglo be nationalised.

- I asked, for the benefit of the room, why we should guarantee existing long-term borrowings of the banks, and they responded in terms of ensuring a consistent message to the market, avoiding market differentiation, the negative reaction that would arise if existing lenders to banks were disadvantaged compared to new, pointing out that addressing the funding situation as it stood would require that existing lenders would also be new lenders.

- Similar arguments arose in relation to subordinated debt, but I do not recall now if the bankers made a distinction between dated and undated subordinate debt. I do not recall any suggestion from any of the official parties at any stage that undated subordinated debt would be covered.[11]

- There was a discussion of how much the banks ought to pay the Government for a guarantee, and Eugene Sheehy suggested a risk-adjusted model such as the American FDIC[12] charging system. This of course would have made the guarantee a very cheap arrangement from a banking perspective and certainly would not be anything like a 'commercial rate' in the circumstances.

It has emerged in the media in recent times that Sean Fitzpatrick had been to visit at least one of these two banks that day, and had asked that the larger bank would take over Anglo. If true, I do not recall this rather salient piece of information being passed on, at least while I was present, in the meeting with the Taoiseach. One would think it should have been.

The bankers left the room, and the meeting continued in the light of their comments. In some ways their interventions had only added colour to the picture of the situation that had already been available to us. Their suggestion that on current trends even the two big banks would run out of funds was in fact more or less self-evident, but their description of that day's market activity was useful, and their pessimism added to the conviction that decisive steps were required.

In fact, theirs was not even a worst-case scenario. In the absence of significant official intervention, a failure of Anglo to meet any of its obligations would trigger events of default on many of its borrowings, so billions of euro would become payable immediately. Anglo's depositors would lose access to their money and the bank would close its doors. Depositors, large and small, would rush to take funds from the other banks, and international investors would withdraw from Ireland as much as they could. Payment systems, such as international credit card and debit card service providers, might withdraw services from their Irish customers abroad, and internationally traded businesses could face impossible demands for upfront payments for goods and services and could no longer rely on their bank guarantees and working capital facilities, as the Irish banks would not have the cash to honour them. The effect of an Anglo default could be exacerbated by the failure within the same week of ILP, and probably all banks would be told to close their doors for days or weeks while authorities struggled to cope. The resulting recession would be unprecedented and the damage to the Irish economy and society would be long term and devastating.

So, in other words, there was never a realistic option for the authorities to step back from the situation and 'let the banks take the hit'. A decision was required and the approach most favoured in the meeting was turning out to be that of granting broad guarantees to all of the significant Irish banks.

How was the guarantee framed? Well, first, there was a discussion on whether to include existing borrowings of the banks and existing deposits within the framework of the guarantee. The question was simple enough in relation to deposits – most were relatively short term, and as soon as they matured would have to be replaced with guaranteed deposits, so a restriction on deposits was not likely to be very advantageous, either in keeping down the size of the Government guarantee or in protecting the deposit base. In relation to bonds of various types, the meeting accepted the bankers' arguments that it was important to keep the bondholders on board to encourage the flow of new funds.

The term – or length of time applicable – for the guarantee was also discussed, and it was decided that two years ought to be enough, and that if problems persisted for longer then other mechanisms would have been found to address issues in the meanwhile. I do not recall anyone arguing for a shorter period, although my notes suggest that the Financial Regulator had a certain minimum period in mind, and indeed given that the tone of the meeting was to make a decisive demonstration of support for the banking system a very short-term guarantee might have been counterproductive.

And there was a relatively short discussion, too, about the question of whether to include dated subordinated debt within the guarantee. Earlier, I referred briefly to a meeting on 26 September, at which the available range of options was discussed, and a paper was presented by the Merrill Lynch team. There had been a discussion on precisely this question at that meeting, and some of the Merrill team had felt – on balance – that inclusion of dated subordinated debt[13] in any broad guarantee was warranted. When asked at the meeting on 29/30 September about what the advice had been on this issue, I was able to recount the 26 September discussion, and so dated subordinate debt was in. I do not know, of course, what the decision would have been if I had reported a different view from the 26 September meeting.

At some stage later in the evening, David Doyle, seeing my unease, asked me directly my view on the appropriate approach to be taken. I did not know then, and do not know now, what was the best approach – indeed, there are so many counterfactual possibilities to be considered that I think that question can never be answered. The broad guarantee as granted, or with adjustments, might well have been the best decision to take. However, that was not my recommendation on the night in question.

I addressed the Taoiseach directly (I am not sure if Minister Lenihan was in the room at the time; I certainly don't remember any reaction from him on this point). I said that in my view we should 'take Anglo out', meaning that Anglo should be taken over by the State, that there would have to be guarantees granted to keep Anglo funded, and that we should make soft guarantees in relation to the other banks. By soft guarantee I meant that we should make solemn assurances to the market about the support the Government was prepared to give to the banking system, but not to make them legally binding.

The Taoiseach was not disposed to entertain my views on this, either then or later when I reminded him that if there were to be a nationalisation it would take some hours to organise, so that any such decision would have to be taken as quickly as possible. It is not possible to say whether the approach I recommended would have been any better than that which was in the end followed. What was certain was that there were huge risks which had to be addressed in a decisive way. My recommendation, which I think more or less mirrored the views of Merrills and the NTMA, might have provided a better outcome if it bought some time for Ireland while a European approach to the crisis was developed (and there was no way of knowing how likely that might be at the time), and if the market was sufficiently reassured by the 'soft' guarantee to provide funding to the other Irish banks in the meanwhile. In that case, the less comprehensive 'soft' guarantees involved might have allowed more freedom for manoeuvre at a later stage in negotiating with bondholders for bail-ins, for example, and the lesser guarantees might have excited less negative comment in other European states, the UK in particular.

On the other hand, if my approach had been adopted, and deposit withdrawals from the other banks had continued, we would probably have had to announce the nationalisation of Anglo on the Tuesday, then do the same again for ILP on the Thursday – or adopt the broad guarantee approach at that stage.

But it is important to remember that the question for the meeting at that stage was not which options might on balance be the best and least costly. So long as there was a risk – and there certainly was one – of a real economic disaster in the following days, the question became which approach had the best chance of staving that off. Each of us, I am sure, was concerned that a mis-step that night could lead to closed ATM machines, lost cash, lost jobs and huge disruption to the lives of our community in a matter of hours or days.

So it is easy in retrospect to analyse the situation and say there were better options. On the night, or indeed for some time beforehand, finding the neatest, most elegant, cheapest option was, well, rather beside the point.

The question of how the State would charge the banks for its guarantee was also discussed. I was privately a bit horrified by one or two suggestions which seemed to me to err towards too light a burden, relative to the State's risk, but did not have to object because there was a quick agreement that this could not be decided until later, and that the banks would simply have to accept that the guarantee would come with a 'yet to be quantified' cost.

But even if a broad guarantee for all the significant institutions was to be agreed – as was by late evening more or less clearly going to be the case – there were huge potential obstacles in making it 'stick', and much discussion that evening focussed on this point.

Guarantees entail a 'credit' enhancement: the lenders' belief, or 'credit', that they will be repaid is enhanced by the attachment to the loan of a guarantee from a more creditworthy party. For a guarantee to be effective, the lender must believe it to be valid or legally granted, and they must believe in the intent and ability of the guarantor to deliver on it, at least within the range of likely circumstances in which it could be called upon. It is not a confidence 'trick', but a real commitment. However, its effectiveness in allowing the banks to raise funds and protect against further losses of deposits is entirely dependent on the confidence that depositors and money and bond market participants would place in it.

So it would be quite possible to give a guarantee and see it fail immediately, if some circumstance arose which would undermine that market confidence. This was especially the case since there would be a short period – even if only a day or two – when the guarantee would really only be a statement of the Government's intent, because it could not come into law until the Oireachtas had enacted the necessary legislation, and it had been passed and signed by the President. Any serious challenge to the validity of the proposed guarantee, especially in that period, could leave the Government in the dreadful position of having bound itself to back the banks' funding but without actually improving their funding position.

The biggest likely danger to the validity of the guarantee came from within the State aid rules of the European Union, which prevent Governments from supporting businesses to the detriment of competitors from other countries, thus ensuring a more level playing field and a fairer commercial market place. So support to banks was normally illegal, and a guarantee given illegally would not attract market confidence.

To be accepted in the market, the Irish guarantee had to clearly fit within the exceptions to the normal rules, the most important being the exception which may apply in circumstances of a serious disturbance in the economy of a member state, and even then cannot be regarded as being given carte blanche. Moreover, the guardian of the State aid rules is the European Commission, and it has very wide powers to circumscribe State aid activities by governments, even in emergencies. Worse, it would not be possible to arrange a State aid 'clearance' from the Commission in the time required, so we would have to rely on making the correct legal judgments, then working with the Commission to ensure retrospectively that we stayed within the rules.[14]

So it would be essential that neither the Commission, nor any senior European official, or indeed any other Government would seriously question the validity of the guarantee. Even serious speculation about its validity could render it ineffective, if that speculation was treated seriously in the market. More than that, any serious danger, at least as perceived by the markets, that the guarantee legislation would not be passed would also render it ineffective.

Finally, the market had to believe that Ireland would do everything possible to protect its banking system to avoid calls on the guarantee, since it was clearly not possible for Ireland to pay out on every possible obligation in the event that all the banks would fail at once. The confidence inspired by the guarantee was as much a product of the perceived willingness to avoid bank defaults as it was a product of the insurance granted to the lenders and depositors in the event of default. The guarantee, therefore, was a fragile thing, especially in the first few days.

I recall expressing these concerns, with the strong support of Paul Gallagher, the Attorney General, several times that evening. The Attorney General was a very clear thinker, and he had had these issues in mind throughout the discussion. He would have the task of making sure all our actions were legally as watertight as possible, and of preparing our legal position for the discussions with the Commission, and he was steering the discussion to ensure the legalities were addressed. But effort would also have to be expended not only on ensuring the actual legal validity, but also the perceived validity among market participants. On one of my later interventions on this point, Minister Lenihan, possibly thinking I was overplaying my concerns, asked who would wish to challenge the guarantee. I replied that any of the market participants who were to be excluded from the protection of the guarantee might decide it was to their advantage to be troublesome. On this I was correct, as we discovered quite soon.

I think it is sometimes imagined that on the night of 29 September that year there was a single meeting, with certain bankers present, at which the fateful decision to guarantee large parts of the banking system was made. In fact, as I hope I have made clear, there was a rolling series of discussions, with some changing personae, in the meeting room occupied by the Taoiseach. Of course the people outside in the corridors and waiting rooms, and indeed in other buildings in Merrion Street and Dame Street, were engaged in their own discussions and preparations. There were breaks, side discussions, interruptions and so forth.

One such interruption, to give an example, came when Joe Lennon, one of the Taoiseach's advisers, came in to the meeting room to break the news that in the US Congress the TARP plan – which was intended to save their banking system and economy and, by the way, also reduce the contagion effects for Europe – had failed to pass the Congress. This was just one of many pieces of bad news to cope with that dreadful day, but it had some real implications for the process in Government Buildings. The first was that the money markets were likely to be even more unsettled the next few days, adding to the pressure for really decisive action in Ireland that night. The other was that markets which had been, quite literally, banking on one Government-announced initiative passing a parliamentary process had been disappointed, and that might leave them less inclined to accept an announcement by the Irish Government at face value, until all the parliamentary processes had been completed.

Joe's interruption was not the only one – there were stops while the bankers were moved in and out at particular times, and probably for other purposes too, throughout the night. I have a vague recollection of someone pouring tea, at some stage, and as I already mentioned, there was a side meeting between the Taoiseach and the Minister for Finance. I have also noted that I left the room myself once or twice to consult colleagues outside and, at a distance, the Merrill's team.

But once the main decision to grant the broad guarantee had been made, the level of movement in and out of rooms and corridors went up considerably. There was a lot to be arranged:

- The press release, in which the key elements of the decision would be formulated and presented, had to be drafted.

- Preparations had to be made for an incorporeal Government Meeting – a consultation of Government members and decision to be taken by telephone.

- Work had to commence on adapting the legislation already drafted to the specifics of the new decision.

- Arrangements had to be made for the contingency that the guarantee announcement would not be immediately effective, and therefore to have other processes in place to ensure that Anglo in particular, but also ILP, could be provided with funds when they opened for business a few hours later, or in the following days.[15]

- Question and answer points and press briefing had to be developed for the next morning.

- Preparations had to be made for breaking the news to our international partners first thing the next morning, especially to forestall any statements from them that might undermine the acceptability of the guarantee in the market.

- All the institutions concerned had to be contacted and told to put their own contingency arrangements into place.

- There was paperwork to be done; for example, the Central Bank lending to Anglo, which had already started that day, required a letter of comfort from the Minister for Finance to the Central Bank, and the form of words had to be agreed and the letter signed by Lenihan.

There was, in other words, a lot of work yet to be done that night.

One particular concern to me was the instruction I had received for the drafting of the press statement and government decision. As I was sent out to start drafting, I was told to stick as closely as possible to the drafting suggested by the banks, since this was their area of expertise, and we wished to avoid any misinterpretations or legal/definitional problems.

I thought, however, that the wording suggested by the bankers was at best likely to be less clear, and at worst would have a different meaning, to that which we intended. After a few minutes at the keyboard of Joe Lennon's computer, to which he had kindly given me access, I was sure that I could not reconcile my understanding of the decision the authorities intended to take with the wording that was suggested.

I went looking for the Taoiseach (I think, but am not sure at this stage, that the Minister for Finance had already left to make his own preparations for the next morning). I told the Taoiseach that I thought the bankers' wording was inappropriate, even disingenuous, and I said to him that if we used it, 'the bankers will be in there laughing at us', or words very close to that. I explained that I felt that without changes we would be committed to guarantees still broader and longer lasting than we intended. The Taoiseach took the point, and the drafting from that point on was our own.

In fact, the decision/press release went through, probably, a dozen drafts, each one mostly only a little different to the previous, before it was finalised. Not only did the wording of the guarantee have to be precise enough for financial markets, but the decision had to be properly framed to reflect the need to justify the action within the EU State aid rules discussed above.

I might just note at this point that while there is a good deal of consistency among witnesses at the Banking Inquiry on the basic facts of what happened that night, there have been some differences in the detail. I cannot reconcile them all and do not feel that I need to – this is my perspective and, having checked my facts where I could, this is how I recall those events. Moreover, all of the people in Government Buildings that evening had their part to play, so naturally there will be elements of their stories not reflected in mine.

3.

Breaking the News –
Morning, 30 September 2008

A s the various groups dispersed to do their work, I went back to my office and scribbled out a list of people whom I would have to telephone the next morning, and I think a list for the Secretary General and Minister also, though I am sure they had their own. By now there was no chance I would be able to go home for a change of clothes, so I parked myself on a couch on the first floor landing of the Department of Finance premises in Government Buildings – from past experience I knew it was more comfortable than sleeping on my desk, which in any event was covered with papers I would need in the morning. I hoped that the soldiers who patrol these buildings at night would not disturb me, and I closed my eyes for 20 minutes or so. In that regard, I think I did better than William Beausang and his team, who were straight into work on adapting the legislation. Indeed, I doubt if they got much of a chance to sleep over the next few days.

Quite a few people have by now written or spoken about their immediate reactions to Brian Lenihan's telephone calls that morning, for example, Joan Burton,[16] Enda Kenny,[17] Christine Lagarde,[18] Neelie Kroes[19] and Alistair Darling,[20] and there is little point in my adding to their accounts except to say that Lenihan's descriptions of these phone calls at the time was a little more upbeat than their recollections. But he was in the moment, working away on behalf of his country, a little bit nervous I think, quite excited, and very anxious to get it right. And it was, indeed, a success to get through those phone calls without anyone attempting actually to call a halt to the guarantee decision, for the reason explained earlier – that even a hint of a legal challenge from any of the big players might scupper the whole thing. So he was entitled to be somewhat upbeat.

I would note though a little disappointment about Alistair Darling's later comments, along the lines that he or others ought to have been consulted beforehand. I met Darling the following St Patrick's Day, when I accompanied Lenihan to meet him at 11 Downing Street, the official residence of Britain's Chancellors of the Exchequer since Georgian times, and he was pleasant, professional and generous with his time and thoughts. But I think that when he made those later comments he could have found it in himself to be a little more understanding of the position Lenihan had been in at the time of the guarantee. When Darling was in a similar position himself not so many days later, facing the likely collapse of an enormous British-headquartered international banking group, RBS, no one from Darling's office picked up the telephone to consult Ireland, even though the fate of RBS' subsidiary, Ulster Bank, would be of huge importance to us (more on this later). The fact was that in the absence of a European system for dealing with these issues, each country was more or less on its own. Just as Darling did not have time for consulting Ireland on RBS some days later – he was too busy rescuing his banking system – Ireland could not realistically have consulted everyone else that might have liked to be included in the discussions on the guarantee decision.[21]

My own series of telephone calls went more or less as expected. One of my first calls was to the *chef de cabinet* in Neelie Kroes' office, Anthony Whelan. In the European Commission, a *chef de cabinet*, or 'head of office', is like a personal chief of staff working closely with the Commissioner in getting his or her political agenda achieved. As such they are key contact points and can often advise informally on matters which will be the subject of a formal approach to the Commission and its permanent staff. Kroes is a very able woman, well liked and highly respected, and in her role as Competition Commissioner at the time, her decisions would make or break the chances of the guarantee 'sticking'. Whelan was very helpful, and I told my bosses afterwards that he gave good advice on how to proceed with the Commission services; he had flashed lots of yellow warning lights, but no red lights (or so I thought at the time – I wonder what would be his own evaluation now). Kroes herself was said to be 'hopping mad' in an email I saw that day from a colleague in the Department of the Taoiseach, but the official position of the Commission was simply that they expected to get details of our intervention shortly, and would study it for adherence to State aid rules. Thankfully, there was no attempt to stop us in our tracks.

I also made contact very early on with Irmfried Schwimann. Dr Schwimann is a senior European Commission official whom I had previously dealt with a few years earlier during the Irish EU Presidency – back then she was working in a different part of the Commission on bank regulation, and I wondered if the fact that she was now working on State aids indicated that the Commission was beefing up its team dealing with State interventions in banking systems. As I recall, that afternoon I received an email from a woman who had been appointed, by Dr Schwimann I presume, to formally open a State aid case for Ireland's banks – the opening correspondence of many years of close engagement between the Commission State aids teams and Ireland's banking issues. These people were to be very important in shaping our crisis responses, and their opening salvoes were professional and understanding, if also concerned.

Also of significance and real concern were my contacts that day with the UK Treasury. It did not take long for them to form the view that any decision favouring Irish banks should also apply to UK banks in Ireland. Clive Maxwell, a senior official who had battled through the Northern Rock issues – incidentally being quite helpful in ensuring that Irish customers of Northern Rock could be reassured that their deposits were safe – was now asking whether the 'subsidiaries' mentioned in our press release as also to be covered by the guarantee was a reference to the Irish subsidiaries of UK banks.

Also that day, or the next, at the suggestion of my colleague Jim O'Brien, our representative on the important Economic and Financial Committee, I took a call from two Commmission officials, one of whom later was a key actor in the Commission's interventions in the Greek problems, and the other of whom was later one of the European Commission's team in the negotiations with Ireland on its rescue programme. They asked me why there were no phone calls to the Commission or other member states from Ireland before the guarantee decision was made. I simply noted that banks and banking systems were failing throughout the EU, but that Ireland had received no phone calls about any one of them. 'The system does not work,' they said, I thought more to each other than to me.[22]

Of course, at many different levels Irish politicians and officials busied themselves explaining the situation to their counterparts in Brussels and in European capitals. The guarantee's success was dependent on the acquiescence, if not the active support, of these people.

Meanwhile, of course, everyone was worried about whether the guarantee would actually work – would the outward flow of funds dry up or even reverse. There was no certainty about this, and the various teams of officials had continued to work on the assumption that it might not. There were a number of strands of possible intervention in preparation:

- Even before the bankers had left Government Buildings in the early hours of that morning – Tuesday, 30 September 2008 – they had been asked to participate in liquidity support for Anglo if required.

- At 4.00 that morning, a final or near final version of a 'collateralised liquidity swap' arrangement was produced. A CLS arrangement – similar to some arrangements used in the UK and elsewhere – would swap government bonds, which could easily be submitted as collateral for Central Bank funds, and which would therefore have given the banks access to funding from that source, in return for apparently valuable but non-eligible assets which could not be used directly at the Central Bank.

- The NTMA was also ready to make direct loans if directed to do so; all the paperwork was ready to go.

- Similarly, the Central Bank had arrangements in place to make limited direct loans to Anglo.

So there was no doubt that the authorities had the resources and the systems ready to make huge interventions to support the banking system – quite apart from the guarantee – and indeed the legislation being put in place was drafted to allow for a wide range of different types of supports.

Banks, however, are not normal businesses: they are the repository of the cash resources of most of the economy, and for that reason, and sometimes also because they are over-exposed to short-term money markets, they have huge liabilities that can they can be called upon to repay with only short periods of notice, or none. Even depositors whose money is on term deposit may be legally entitled to demand access to their funds with only a small interest penalty. So in the face of an all-out run on a banking system the size of Ireland's, it could well be the case that even a very large contingency fund would last only for a few days or a couple of weeks. So it was very important that the guarantee should work.

Meanwhile, there was a frenzy of legislative drafting and other activity in the Department of Finance and the Attorney General's Office. The plan was to have the Bill presented to the Houses of the Oireachtas by, if I recall correctly, Wednesday afternoon, to allow for legal effect to be given to the decision taken early on Tuesday morning.

However, early on Tuesday afternoon, or perhaps it was late in the morning, I met the Minister as I stepped out of a meeting in the main conference room in the Department of Finance office on Merrion Street. He seemed irritated, telling me that no one seemed to be acting as if the Bill would be in the Dáil that day. I was surprised that he would say this, as this was not the plan.

'But I agreed this with the Attorney General an hour ago,' was the Minister's response.

'Minister,' I asked, 'did you or the Attorney tell anyone after you made the decision?'

ьenihan paused, smiled for a brief moment, then said stern-ly, 'well, you know now'.

But actually it was good news that we were forced to save a day on this process – speed was of the essence, as the faster the legislation could be passed, the less likely the guarantee would be questioned in the market.

In fact, market participants and advisers took the guarantee more or less at face value that day.

- Credit rating agencies made positive assessments about the impact of the guarantee on the banking system.

- Ireland's AAA credit rating was left unchanged.

- Credit default swap markets showed a clear improvement as far as bank credits were concerned, and only a relatively small, but significant, negative effect for Irish sovereign credit.

- Most commentators were relatively positive, some noting that the guarantee had yet to be checked against the State aids rules, but not challenging the validity of the scheme in general.

Most importantly of all, monies did start to return to the banks that day. Our report from Anglo that evening said that they had raised a net €2.8 billion in funds that day from a fairly wide variety of sources. In the short term, at least, the guaran-tee was working.

After an emergency passage through both Houses of the Oireachtas, the Bill became law on Friday, 3 October 2008. That was exactly four weeks after that first phone call about trouble at Irish Nationwide.

That was some four weeks.

Competitors demand access to the guarantee

I have already indicated that the UK authorities were very quick to suggest that subsidiaries of UK banks in Ireland should be able to avail of the guarantee. In fact, there was quite broad international pressure both to extend the guarantee to other banks and to ensure that Irish banks using the guarantee would not siphon away liquidity from banks in other places which had no formal guarantee. All we could do was explain the depth of our problems, noting that if we had not addressed them decisively, the impact on the rest of Europe would have been a lot worse – a point which was almost certainly true.

Of course, the Irish guarantee initiative was not the only one. On the far side of the EU, Slovenian banks were, it was being said, losing funds to Austrian banks, after the Austrian Government had promised to make sure that depositors were fully covered (though this was a promise, not a legal guarantee, as I recall) and in France, Germany and other places similar solemn assurances had been given by Governments. While the Irish guarantee was not the cause of their difficulties, some of the authorities of these countries resented it as being 'unfair', though of course they had not consulted us before entering into their own less formal arrangements. Still, no new friends had been made that week, and the Irish Government was on the back foot in terms of its relations with its neighbours. This was especially the case, of course, as far as the UK was concerned, where the chief executives of two big Scottish-based banks were no doubt spending a great deal of effort in decrying the Irish efforts to the Chancellor and Prime Minister. It seems certain, now, that their quite substantial market problems – especially those of RBS – were being blamed at least in part on the Irish guarantee, even though the depths of their own difficulties were to become clear very shortly.

Discussions with Neelie Kroes, advice on the guarantee legislation received from the ECB and ongoing contacts with the UK and other countries all made plain that a flat refusal to allow, especially, UK bank subsidiaries into the scheme would be very difficult to make. In fact, a formal decision was made to allow certain of these subsidiaries to apply to join the scheme, but there would have to be extra conditionality to ensure that the guarantee could be properly policed and maintained in such cases.

The situation came to a head somewhat at the ECOFIN meeting of 7 October 2008, which took place in Luxembourg. As noted, the UK had been piling on the pressure for the Irish guarantee to include the Irish subsidiaries of UK banks. Their legal position was probably strong in this regard – one could not discriminate against these subsidiaries on grounds of nationality. However, the guarantee was already covering a huge range of liabilities, and there was a concern that each addition made it more difficult to maintain the integrity of the guarantee in the eyes of the market. More importantly, a guarantee from the Irish Government to these subsidiaries might be used by the banks concerned to support their headquarters' liquidity requirements, or might provide an incentive for those headquarters to provide less intergroup funding to the Irish operations. In other words, the incentives were all wrong. Worse, however poor the information available on Irish banks' asset positions, we had no way of checking on the soundness of the UK banks, other than to rely on the UK authorities.

While there seemed to Lenihan to be no choice but to go down the route of allowing the guarantee in some cases, he could not do so without some reassurance that it would not be called upon. The plan was to speak to Darling at the ECOFIN that day and extract from him a political commitment in that regard.[23]

In fact, Darling was quite distracted.[24] The RBS share price was plunging and the UK Government was having to make supportive statements to the media. It was a bad day for him to be in Brussels, but had he rushed back to London that in itself might have been taken as a signal of trouble. Lenihan and I eventually caught up with him and one of his officials in a corridor, and spoke for a few minutes. Darling gave a formulaic reassurance – 'no one need worry about the security of RBS', or words to that effect.

Coming away, Lenihan asked me what I thought.

I said, 'I think RBS is in very big trouble but he can't say so – they intend to protect it'.

Lenihan said, 'That's what I think, too'. Political reassurance or not, the Minister was in no hurry to guarantee RBS subsidiaries after that.

Eventually, this situation resolved itself, because the Irish side would not relent on the strength of the conditionality that would apply to banks covered by the guarantee, and to the banking groups to which they belonged. In the end, the UK banks (and indeed the Irish subsidiary of Belgian bank KBC), did not want to, or were not allowed to, accept the types of conditions that accompanied the guarantee as it applied to Irish banks, including cross-guarantees within the groups and an entitlement of the Irish authorities to intervene in the management of the groups concerned. We heard from one of these banks, for example, that their financial regulator would not countenance the level of Irish control that would be entailed. Presumably, too, the steps the UK took to rescue their banks made access to the Irish guarantee much less important.

National Irish Bank, which despite the name was actually a branch operation of the Danish Danske Bank, had also raised concerns about its position almost immediately – in fact, even before 9.00 a.m. on the morning the guarantee was announced – as the availability of Government guarantees to all of its main Irish competitors put it in a very difficult spot *vis a vis* its deposit base. However, as a part of a Danish institution, it was shortly to be covered by the wide guarantees offered by the Danish Government to its banks, and it did not seek Irish protection after that.[25]

A few of the Irish subsidiaries of very large international banks also sought to be covered by the Irish guarantee. They say 'any port in a storm' but for these institutions to seek the protection of the Irish guarantee was like an oil tanker seeking shelter in a tiny fishing harbour. Were they really as desperate as this action suggests? In any case, there was no way in which Ireland could extend its guarantee that far. For a few weeks, though, I had a small pile of letters on my desk from various banks not initially covered by the guarantee asking that they be covered as well.

4.

Europe Acts

The meeting in Paris of Heads of State and Government, with all its impressive pomp described earlier, was taking place on Sunday, 12 October 2008, less than two weeks since the European banking system had begun unravelling, giving rise to the necessity for the various bank rescues, including Fortis, Dexia, HRE and the Irish guarantee of six retail banks. In the meanwhile, the UK had had to announce the rescue of RBS, one of the biggest banks in the world, and Iceland's financial and economic system had started to disintegrate.

It turned out to be a tough meeting for Ireland.

For some time before, Irish officials and Irish diplomats had had a lot of explaining to do around Europe, but the Irish guarantee was, so far, well accepted in the market, and even grudgingly admired in one or two places. But it was also evident that some governments had provided background briefings to journalists denigrating the Irish decision and its lack of community spirit. Worse than that, some of those briefings appeared to be deliberately seeking to question the validity and reliability of the guarantee.

By then, I believe I had already spoken to an official in one finance ministry in Europe and was reassured that they were not behind any of this activity, and yet journalists in Brussels had shown an Irish Government press officer a negative briefing document which purported to come from the same country's official system. It could well have been that different parts of a government system were giving different messages, or that some press briefers were not following the official line. Or perhaps in some cases journalists were spinning yarns in the hopes of creating a reaction.

On the other hand, matters had been going well with the State aid experts in the European Commission. William Beausang had been negotiating intensively with them, in close liaison with the legal experts and the Attorney General, and while we had inserted into the draft guarantee scheme various safeguards on which the Commission was insistent, it seemed likely that the EC would accept the most important elements of the Irish initiative, thus making it much more secure from a legal point of view. (In fact, the Commission's positive decision was announced on Monday, 13 October).

Moreover, having been outwardly relatively quiet only a couple of weeks before, the European Commission, and the European Union more generally, were erupting with new initiatives and new responses to the crisis. In the first 10 days of October, the Commission had proposed new rules on bank capital requirements, and the ECOFIN council had launched a new initiative to protect economic growth in Europe. Central Banks had cut interest rates on a co-ordinated basis. Commission President Barroso had launched a new group to examine the future of the supervision structure for banks in Europe and globally, and by mid-month arrangements were well under way for further proposals in a range of areas, from accounting standards to minimum deposit protections to crisis co-ordination arrangements.[26] But in at least some of these initiatives the aim was to accelerate the pace of plans for the future, quite appropriately, but it was also necessary to deal with the crisis of today.

That was what the Paris Summit was for. There was a need for a real European approach to the immediate crisis, and to his credit Sarkozy was determined to deliver it. Also to his credit, he invited Gordon Brown to the meeting, because Brown and his team of UK ministers and officials were the ones who had a plan.

Until then, the Eurogroup discussions had been overseen by finance ministers; this meeting of national leaders, prime ministers and presidents was unprecedented. Even more un-precedented was inviting the UK to play a speaking role. As a non-member of the Euro area, the UK had no right of atten-dance, and there was a protocol difficulty in inviting Brown but not the other non-Euro area leaders. Equally, there were protocol, and no doubt practical, difficulties if they were all to be invited. So, like the victim in a murder mystery, Brown would have the most important role in the first act, but no speaking part afterwards. He would introduce his ideas, give a short presentation, then leave the room to the Euro area lead-ers for their discussion.

Brown outlined the seriousness of the situation in Europe and globally, even noting that a certain significant bank would probably be next to require a rescue, to be announced shortly, indicating the need for a concerted European approach to the crisis situation. He then outlined his suggestions as to what that approach should be.

Brown in effect was proposing that the mixed approach of providing capital to banks, together with the provision of ex-tensive state guarantees for medium-term bond issues, would be adopted as the European standard approach, and that there would be a common expression of the intention to proceed on this basis.

Finally, here was a European initiative that really could address the banking problems. It was two weeks too late to be of use in the Irish case (and perhaps it would not have been sufficient for Ireland), and was far from being a joint initiative with European level financing and implementation, but this was a real step forward. The UK and French authorities, and no doubt quite a few others who had been involved, later got less credit than they deserved.

But for Ireland the devil was in the detail, and the rest of the meeting became a very unpleasant one for us. At that stage, Ireland needed three things from this meeting:

- First, steps had to be taken to underpin stability in the European banking system.

- Second, whatever the outcome for other countries, the approach taken by Ireland in relation to its banking problems should not be undermined by other initiatives.

- Third, already highly stretched, Ireland should not be obliged to enter into new initiatives for which it did not have the resources.

Incomplete and imperfect as it was, the new European initiative had to be regarded as positive in relation to the first of these requirements, the underpinning of broader stability. But the second two were more problematic. On the one hand, the new initiative took quite a different shape to the Irish broad guarantee approach, and we needed to be sure that the broad guarantee was not being called into question. On the other, the proposal seemed to commit countries to rescuing their banks, yet Ireland had already stretched itself to guarantee six banks based in Ireland, with the potential addition of a number of

Irish subsidiaries of banks based in other European countries. There had to be some limit to our obligations. Perhaps the proposal should refer to the rescue only of systemically important banks.

The Taoiseach made these points, but got no comfort – the body language and tone from other leaders were quite negative.

He tried again, explaining why these issues were important for Ireland, and why an unravelling of the Irish situation would be bad for Europe. Again, the tone and content of responses, including from Sarkozy in the chair, were negative. Trichet, from whom we had hoped for some support, did not help, as he underlined that in order to give the ECB the freedom of movement it wanted for the operation of monetary policy, the guarantees provided under the new initiative should never cover short-term paper. The Irish guarantee was already covering short-term deposits and bills of all kinds. The Danes would have been useful allies, having recently announced a broad guarantee of their own, but Denmark was not in the Euro area, so they were not in attendance.

Cowen kept battling on, insisting that Irish points be heard, despite an apparently deaf ear from some of Europe's most powerful people ranged around the room.

Thankfully, there was a lunch break, which allowed for the possibility to lobby the participants and try to make some progress on a personal basis where little had been possible in the meeting room. The Taoiseach had his own counterparts to meet, and I went in search of officials with whom I was acquainted who might be helpful. As far as I recall, I tried but did not manage to get hold of Jorg Asmussen, the senior German Finance Ministry official dealing with banking matters. I did speak to David Vegara, the head of the Spanish Finance

Ministry and also chairman of the Financial Services Committee of which I was a member. It was he, I think, who gave me some good advice: this was Sarkozy's meeting and Sarkozy was well served by one or two personal advisers. It was they who could influence the final outcome.

So I found Sarkozy's economic advisor and asked him why he thought the discussion was so difficult – we were only trying to protect our position and it seemed as if it would be easy to accommodate us. On the issue of not undermining our existing guarantee, he was reassuring. The language had to speak of a common approach, but no one, certainly not Sarkozy, was suggesting any unwinding of the Irish guarantee.

On the question of our request, though, to limit interventions to more important institutions, he expressed his surprise at our stance. 'But you have already guaranteed all of your banks'. I explained that no, we had not; there were plenty of small credit institutions and, more importantly, medium-sized international banks which we could not afford to support and which had not been covered by our guarantee. Why should it be a problem for anyone else to say that only significant banks should be covered, I wondered.

Because at least one big country had lots of small banks which it might wish to rescue, if it came to it, but which might not be regarded as meeting the threshold of systemically important, was the answer.

I don't recall what the Taoiseach told me of his lunchtime efforts, but at least we had a better understanding of what the obstacles were as the afternoon progressed.

The meeting after lunch went a little better for us, I think, perhaps assisted by the discussions which had taken place earlier. The elegantly presented after-lunch cigars graciously offered to the political leaders ranged around the meeting room might have been refused by a large majority of them, but while I knew nothing of Mrs Merkel's stance on smoking, I thought that the big puffs of cigar smoke coming from whichever prime minister was sitting next to her would certainly not have helped my mood, if I had been sitting there.

Just as the chairman was trying to wind up the meeting, Cowen spoke up again. He had to be clear that no one was going to suggest, even by implication, any change in the Irish guarantee arrangement. The response was impatient but helpful – what has gone before is unaffected, this initiative is in relation to new situations, and no one would say differently.

Usually these types of meetings are followed immediately by a press conference. The chairperson of the meeting and the appropriate senior figures – the head of the Eurogroup, the Presidents of the Commission and of the ECB, for example – are expected to appear together in front of the cameras and present the main conclusions of the meeting, almost as soon as it has ended. Officials follow the debate and draft speaking points for the chairperson, taking note of any last minute changes during the discussion. We waited long enough to listen to the press conference to be sure that if any point arose in relation to Ireland we would be aware of it, and ready to reply if need be. Then we headed back to the airport.

On the flight back that evening we all seemed a bit bruised and tired, but the Taoiseach lightened the mood. He is a good mimic, and had been Minister for Foreign Affairs, so he gave those of us sitting in the small aircraft a five minute performance of an imagined comical discussion between various world leaders he had known. On a couple of them his imitation was so close you could almost close your eyes and imagine they were in the cabin.

5.

Capitalisation and Nationalisation

That was a Sunday. All the Irish authorities were still very busy putting the scaffolding around the guarantee. The legislation required that support of credit institutions would take place in accordance with a scheme which itself had to be presented to the Oireachtas, and each institution would have to be covered by a deed of guarantee, which would not only provide for the guarantee, but give extensive rights of oversight to the authorities, as well as providing obligations and limits which would apply to the banks. The hectic pace of work that had continued since early September had not abated, and indeed the requirements of administering the guarantee were adding considerably to the workload. In the Department of Finance a new team of around 20 people, including a helpful mix of 'old hands' and some of the Department's brightest young graduates, would be assigned to provide additional support, and an additional Assistant Secretary, Ann Nolan, would also be assigned to help. But there was no reason for anyone to think that the guarantee had solved any underlying problems. It was best seen as a way to provide additional time for structural solutions to be developed.

On that Wednesday, 15 October 2008, I sent the following message, by email, to my own team, the NTMA, the Financial

Regulator and the Central Bank, as well as the Attorney General's Office and Arthur Cox:

> Some thoughts – we have all been so busy doing the guarantee/Oireachtas processes etc. that there is a danger we will be distracted from preparations for further difficulties. We still have some imbalances out there. I think we need to think about:
>
> A. What recapitalisations might be required?
> B. What consolidations might be required?
> C. Whether any nationalisations might be required?
>
> To leave our system in a stronger position.[27]

I went on to suggest some preparations that might be commenced and suggested a teleconference a couple of days later. I finished with:

> To be clear – there is no Govt policy to recap or to nationalise anything, we are brainstorming scenarios here.

I did not have any policy direction to follow, but it was clear that the guarantee would need to be supplemented by other efforts and we may as well get started, or restarted, since these issues had been discussed to some extent already. Now they would come to the fore. So, even before the ink was dry on the guarantee, Government authorities and their advisers had started to consider the structure and capital position of the banks.

Engaging with the private sector

It is quite normal when banks are in difficulty for authorities – regulators, Central Banks, Governments – to seek to arrange takeovers and mergers within their banking systems, using

77

the strengths of some banks to compensate for the weaknesses of others, in ways which protect customers, the public purse and overall financial stability. Alternatively, the authorities might seek to encourage outside investors to put money into the banking system, underpinning its ability to deal with losses and providing external pressure on management to realign the business in more profitable directions. When these neat private sector solutions can be arranged, and done well, they allow for the burden of adjustment in the banking sector – or much of it – to rest with the private sector and for the public purse to be protected. Ireland was not going to work out like that, however.

Why not? Well, imagine a situation in which Bank A has plenty of capital, and is well funded and profitable, but wishes to extend its customer base to a new business or geographical sector. Bank A also wants to operate within a stable and efficient financial system. Bank B has a liquidity problem and a good amount of bad debts, but has good access to the kind of customers that Bank A would like to have more of, and with appropriate restructuring can produce real profit-generating opportunities. In this type of circumstance, a little official encouragement and help could be used to push for a merger between the two banks – the shareholders in Bank B will probably (and quite properly) take a loss, but overall financial stability will be boosted and the public purse will avoid taking on the burden of rescuing Bank B.

In Ireland at the end of 2008, however, there were no such 'marriages made in heaven' possible between banks. As we discovered in September 2008, even the largest banks were vulnerable from a liquidity point of view and market participants were increasingly sceptical about their capital adequacy in the face of potential losses, and were also increasingly expecting banks in general to have higher levels of capital than before. So despite exploring various potential linkages, there were no good matches to be made between Irish banks to reduce overall risks within the system. None of the banks was strong enough, in other words, to take on the problems of another without risking damage to its own position.

What about outside investment? There was no shortage of private investors expressing an interest in the Irish banks in the last three months of 2008, and the banks were strongly encouraged by the Irish authorities to explore whatever avenues there were for raising private capital.

Various private equity houses and other investor groups were expressing interest in making or brokering investments. Groups such as TPG and KKR – large private equity concerns – were exploring opportunities in Ireland, while there were some local initiatives also. A group calling itself 'Mallabraca', with links to international investors with deep pockets, was showing a very active interest in investing in Irish banks, mostly at the time in Bank of Ireland. And there seemed to be some real interest by a mostly Irish consortium coordinated by Deutsche Bank in investing in the Irish banking system.

There was also a constant stream of other, usually smaller, financial and consultancy firms seeking to engage with the Government and the banks. David McWilliams, the well-known economist and commentator, for example, brought a small Swiss investment bank into the Department of Finance on a number of occasions to explore particular business opportunities. As previously discussed, McWilliams had been giving advice to Ministers, including Brian Lenihan in advance of the guarantee, so it was not surprising that Lenihan would be happy to meet him again later, though for various reasons no business was concluded with this group.

All of these potential investment opportunities had to be considered by the Minister for Finance and the banks themselves, so many of these potential investors, advisers, brokers and the like were engaged with by the Minister and by Department and NTMA officials as appropriate, as well as by the banks involved. This was a time- and resource-consuming effort and it undoubtedly slowed the decision-making process in relation to State capital injections. On the other hand, it would have been wrong to put State funds into the banks if there were private funds available for the purpose.

As it turned out, however, investors were not interested in making straightforward investments in the banks. In most cases the investment proposition was – when finally clarified – based on the State providing not just a liquidity guarantee but also a guarantee against losses. The potential investors wanted – not unreasonably, if you can get such a deal – to leave most of the risk with the State and take most of the upside for themselves. There was no deal offered which looked like good value from the State's perspective.

Meanwhile, the ongoing work of PWC on behalf of the Financial Regulator in investigating the loan books of the banks was making it clear that – even though the outlook was not seen as nearly as dire as later proved to be the case – at least some additional capital would be required by almost all of the banks we were dealing with. Other matters of some concern also surfaced first in the context of the PWC reports.[28]

All of these considerations came together in a series of discussions towards the end of November. These took place first at the Government-owned Farmleigh House, then in a second round of discussions about a week later in the Department of

Finance buildings in Merrion Street. Each bank was brought in, asked to discuss its current position, its capital needs and its future plans, as well as possible tie-ups with other institutions. The Minister for Finance led the discussions and each of the institutions was represented, at least, by its chairperson and chief executive, who responded in their own styles – variously open, friendly, combative or defensive, depending on the individuals concerned.

As the crisis had developed, the Department of Finance was increasingly 'under watch'. There were journalists and cameramen near the Department's main entrance much of the time, often hovering near the front door but occasionally half-hidden in alleyways across the road. Others with a business agenda apparently also watched the building from time to time. Increasingly, meetings in the Minister's conference room, which faced on to Merrion Street and could be seen from across the road, or from the Merrion Hotel opposite, were held with the blinds closed. The idea of going out to Farmleigh was to allow for some space to hold confidential discussions outside the city centre without the pressure of immediate media demands for explanation and response. The early appearance of cameramen at the Farmleigh gate suggested that not everyone invited had been so concerned about the confidentiality of the process.

The discussions were not always the relatively open and honest exchanges of views one might have hoped for – some of the institutions came not only with prepared positions, but with prepared defensive arguments. They were, in some cases, not seeing the reality of their situation, or at least were pretending not to. They did not all accept the need for capital. Some felt they had a significant chance of raising capital themselves, and as a corollary did not accept that the State would soon have to take a stake in the institutions. As late as the second half of October of that year – in other words, just a few weeks before the Farmleigh meetings – Eugene Sheehy had declared that AIB would 'rather die' than take additional capital in the form of equity.[29] In early November, AIB declared that they expected that their capital would remain 'resilient in all plausible scenarios throughout the downturn in the credit cycle'.[30] And now, even with all the dislocation in the capital markets, Dermot Gleeson, the Chairman of AIB, made a passionate statement defending the capital position of AIB, arguing that the State was being misled by its advisers in its understanding of the AIB capital position.

Notwithstanding these claims, it seemed clear to the Minister for Finance and those advising him that the Irish banking system was going to need capital, and that the main provider was likely to be the State. The Government was prepared to insist in its dealing with the banks that capital was required, and after lengthy discussions, the Government announced its proposed approach to recapitalisation (or 'recaps') on 14 December 2008, and the proposed amounts on 21 December 2008 – up to €2 billion each for AIB and Bank of Ireland, and an initial €1.5 billion for Anglo.[31] The amounts of the first capital injections for the banks were in the end somewhat increased beyond what was initially proposed, as it became clear that losses in the banks would be higher than expected. Indeed, these first efforts at recapitalisation would turn out to be just the start of a much more extensive process.

In fact, the capital needs of the banks eventually added up to far more than had been expected in 2008 and early 2009 – total capital injections from the State eventually reached a gross amount of around €64 billion – half of that being attributable to Anglo-Irish bank, but AIB in the end required a total of nearly €21 billion.[32] These were huge sums of money paid by the taxpayer to protect the stability of the financial system, and indirectly the stability of the Irish economy and the well-being of the citizens who saved with and relied on the banking system.

While there have been and will continue to be receipts from the banking system which will directly offset these payments to the banks, and other income arising from the crisis will be received more indirectly, these incoming amounts will not in the end come close to covering the full €64 billion outlay, but it is not possible yet to say what the final figures will be. By mid-July 2015, the State had received about €13 billion in income from the banking sector – the bulk of it related to the sale of stakes in Bank of Ireland and ILP, and fees paid by the banks in return for the bank guarantee. There may be some positive return from the liquidation of IBRC, the entity that was formed from Anglo and INBS, and at the time of writing NAMA is expected to generate a small positive cash return for the State over its life. One might also add in as bank crisis-related income the excess profits of the Central Bank of Ireland, most of which are made available to the State with a one-year time lag, and which are generated in large part by the income the Bank receives on foot of the emergency loans to banks during the crisis.

The biggest remaining variable is probably the State's investment in AIB Bank, where the amount eventually returned to the State will depend on the performance of the bank. It has been suggested that AIB might return the whole amount of the State investment of around €20 billion, but this is speculative. At December 2014, the National Pension Reserve Fund, which holds the State investments in AIB, was valuing its bank assets, mostly AIB, at €13 billion.[33] In December 2015, AIB made a first capital repayment to the State of around €1.6 billion.

One could prudently assume that taking all this into account the final direct net cash cost of the bank interventions will amount to somewhere in the region of €30 to €40 billion, with much still to be determined. Even if it is towards the lower end, this is an enormous sum and excludes both debt servicing and indirect economic costs.

While the biggest generator of capital demands of the Irish banks arose from the performance of its loan book – losses and expected losses on loans made by the banks, in other words – a smaller but not insignificant generator of the recapitalisation requirement was the market and regulatory demand for higher levels of capital for the future. So-called 'Basel III' capital rules, and indeed the Irish Central Bank's own regulatory demands, increased considerably from those which applied in 2008 before the crisis, so the Government's capital injections and other capital-raising measures went not only to meet the costs of bank losses, but also to meet the cost of new, higher regulatory standards.

The private sector also took large losses on its investments in the Irish banks. On top of the €64 billion State investment, the private sector contributed through the loss of money invested in Irish bank shares and in investments in subordinated bonds, which were not repaid in full. I will deal later with issues in relation to so-called 'burden-sharing' or 'burning' of bondholders in the context of discussions around the EU/IMF programme for Ireland, but over the period since September 2008, holders of subordinated bonds of the Irish banks have contributed some €15 billion to bank capital and, depending on how one cares to calculate it, the losses to bank shareholders were also very large.

For financial institutions such AIB, Bank of Ireland and ILP, a corollary of the State capital investment was that with each such investment the ownership stake of the State in the banks increased. Despite efforts to maintain some level of private sector ownership in these institutions, the decline in the value of bank shares and the huge capital investments meant that in most of the institutions concerned the State shareholding quickly dwarfed the private. The State's ownership in AIB, for example, eventually exceeded 99 per cent. In one case, however, there was an early and deliberate decision to insist on full State ownership – that case was Anglo, which was nationalised in January 2009.

Anglo

It was December 2008. As part of the programme of recapitalisations announced for the Irish banks in November and December, it had been decided that Anglo would get some Government money to help in underpinning its capital base against losses. In retrospect, the amounts being discussed seem very small, relative to what we later learnt about the depths of the loan losses that arose in that institution. The final amount of money put into Anglo (and INBS, which was later subsumed into the Anglo structure) amounted to well over €30 billion. But at the time these outlandish figures were not yet known, or perhaps knowable.

Anglo, through its Chief Executive David Drumm and others, had been telling us of their efforts to raise funds from the private sector. They had sounded positive about finding investors to provide some funding, and it was of course essential that any possible private sector investment would be explored. But as we had expected, nothing emerged and it seemed increasingly clear that the only investor was going to be the Government. By 12 December 2008, Anglo's board had decided to formally indicate to the Government that they would need its assistance in raising capital, but remained more optimistic than seemed reasonable in the circumstances, even given the state of knowledge at the time. And the Government would not be willing to make a capital investment in Anglo, or any other bank, without sending in a team to carry out a 'due diligence' exercise.

At meetings with the Department, Drumm presented himself as friendly, helpful, reasonable. No shouting, no apparent impatience. It was a 'let's all work together' type of tone. And he did not, so far as I can recall, ever suggest we should put in the funds without carrying out a due diligence exercise. This is in striking contrast to the tone he struck in internal discussions which were captured on tape and later obtained and published by the Independent Newspapers group in Ireland. In those tapes, as reported in a *Sunday Independent* article of 30 June 2013,[34] he is heard to say on 15 December 2008, in relation to the question of due diligence:

> I'll probably punch him [Lenihan]. And I mean punch him, as if to say, "What are you actually doing?" … "What's this about having to go through due diligence? You made that decision on the 29th of September. You've told the fuckin' world we're all solvent."

So there was a considerable difference between the bluster recorded on the tapes and the performance of the man in the meetings themselves. In fact, one would not recognise one from the other.

So Drumm knew there had to be a due diligence exercise for Anglo, as for the other banks that were to be recapitalised from State funds. But in fact his due diligence was going to be a bit different. Teams of advisers carrying out the exercise would explore some particular practices and events within Anglo, related to the governance of the bank. This did not arise from some particular prejudice in relation to Anglo, but because a range of issues calling into question some of the practices within the bank were already in the public domain. These issues included the mechanisms used for unwinding the large bet that businessman Sean Quinn had made on Anglo's share price, but also the questions around an end-of-financial year deposit transaction involving ILP, and various practices in relation to loans of the Chairman of Anglo.[35]

So the due diligence teams, using resources from PWC, Merrill Lynch and Arthur Cox solicitors, went in to start looking at banking and loan issues, but also at the corporate governance matters. The due diligence confirmed that there were real reasons to be concerned about the governance situation in Anglo.

Even before the due diligence had arisen, Sean Fitzpatrick, David Drumm and Lar Bradshaw felt they should resign from their positions as Chairman, CEO and board member of the bank, respectively. Fitzpatrick came in to the Department of Finance to let us know that arising from aspects of the way the bank's annual results had been presented over the years, in which details of loans from Anglo to its own chairman were not published because they would be repaid before the end of each annual reporting period, then taken out again in the new period, with funds lent by Irish Nationwide being used to bridge the period. Fitzpatrick's own resignation statement said that he had not broken the law, but that his actions lacked the appropriate transparency and that as a result he was resigning.

Lenihan already had a replacement in mind. Donal O'Connor was a member of the Anglo board, but had only been *in situ* for a few months, so could not be regarded as complicit in the loan difficulties or other long-term issues in Anglo. Moreover, O'Connor had one major experience that seemed relevant to current circumstances – he had been put in charge of the wind-up of the assets of Insurance Corporation Ireland, an AIB subsidiary which had gone bust many years before, leading to a State rescue package. Of course, it was not Lenihan's role – at that point – to choose the new chairman of a bank that was not in public ownership, but given that he was about to become by far the biggest shareholder in Anglo, his views were likely to hold sway.

For what it is worth, O'Connor did not, as I recall, dance for joy at the suggestion that he might be made Chairman of the worst bank in Ireland. He was prevailed upon, however, and he took on the task in the public interest and stayed with the bank until mid-2010, when Alan Dukes took over from him. And it quickly became clear that O'Connor would give himself entirely to his new role and be driven by a fiercely strong work ethic. He kept plugging away, and seemed to be devoting himself full-time, rather than giving the part-time attendance that is expected of chairpersons in more usual circumstances.

The Fitzpatrick loan arrangements also were an immediate driving factor behind the resignation of Pat Neary, the CEO of the Financial Regulator. There was evidence that the Regulator, as an organisation, had been aware of the Fitzpatrick loan arrangements since January 2008[36] – in other words, for the best part of a year – and although Mr Neary said clearly that he had not been advised of this, at the time, he resigned on 9 January 2010.

There were other resignations, too, around the same time. Denis Casey and Brian Goggin, CEOs of ILP and Bank of Ireland respectively, resigned around this time, for different reasons. Michael Fingleton stepped down from INBS not long after.

6.

'Unacceptable Practices' and Seeping Liquidity – Anglo is Nationalised

Bank depositors at the retail level tend to leave their money sit. They don't tend to be in and out of their bank branch each month increasing or decreasing their deposits to take account of interest rate movements or day to day newspaper headlines.

Surprisingly, there can also be a good deal of inertia in large wholesale deposits as well, although the very nature of these, often being for short, fixed terms, means that leaving funds with a bank as deposits mature requires an active decision. There comes a point when loss of confidence does start to erode a bank's wholesale and retail deposit base and can accelerate into a bank run.

Anglo had already experienced this to an extent in March 2008 during the scare about their share price. They experienced it again in a nearly disastrous way in September 2008, only being saved by the Government guarantee. And they were now starting to lose funds again in December 2008, despite that guarantee. The negative publicity around the loans to directors, leading to resignations, was unlikely to have helped confidence in the bank, and the authorities were aware that more negative issues were to emerge shortly. How could we

90

expect that market confidence could be maintained, guarantee or not, if Anglo continued to be the source of these unpleasant confidence-shaking revelations? And how could the Government invest capital in Anglo while all of these governance issues persisted? Somehow, it was necessary to press the 'reset' button on Anglo's relationship with the markets and its depositors.

Consequently, the question of fully nationalising Anglo came to the fore again, although it was still an unpleasant option. On the one hand, depositors ought to be reassured by the involvement of the Government. On the other, there were no certainties that, in fact, the bank would be able to fund itself any better as a nationalised entity than in its current status, and the change of ownership might create its own problems, adding to the air of desperation that was already surrounding the bank. But it seemed to be at the very least an option that had to be seriously considered, and so by mid-December the draft legislative provisions to allow for bank nationalisations, which had been ready but not used in September, were being dusted off and checked over.

On 12 December, Merrill Lynch had laid out the pros and cons of an Anglo nationalisation. They were arguing that Anglo was mostly a property-based bank, a business model that was not now going to be sustainable, and that there were going to be losses to be absorbed on its property loans. Nationalisation would at least give the Government clearer control of the Anglo situation and might also, for technical reasons, reduce the amount of capital it had to hold, and therefore the amount that the Government would put in. Advice from the NTMA supported this point of view.

In the end, though, the decision to nationalise was not made until mid-January. Even if the authorities had wanted to

nationalise Anglo in December (and some of the people concerned clearly advised that) there were pragmatic reasons for
a short delay:

1. The necessary legislation would have to be adopted by the
    Government and proposed to the Dáil. While this could
    be done quite quickly in theory, in practice the Christmas
    holidays created some risks – in particular, calling the
    Oireachtas back during a break might be regarded as sig-
    nalling much greater problems to the markets than was in
    fact the case, and create some level of panic.

2. The second consideration was that the due diligence re-
    ports would not be ready until around the second week
    of January, and we would by then have more information
    about the flows of funds, and greater insight into the bank,
    which might affect the official response to Anglo's ongoing
    problems.

So no decision on nationalisation was made in December
and in the meanwhile the plan to recapitalise Anglo, rather
than nationalise it, remained the default option.

As in September 2008, however, so it was in January 2009:
matters were being brought to a head by liquidity pressures.
Anglo had, for a number of weeks, been trading on a narrow
end-of-day liquidity cushion, often of less than a billion euro.
The publicity around the transparency/governance issues, and
the resulting loss of a chairman, CEO and other executive and
non-executive directors, had also alerted investors and depositors to Anglo's continuing difficulties. Bank of Ireland and AIB
might be willing to provide some funding to Anglo since it
was guaranteed by the State, but they were not themselves so
flush that they could make open-ended commitments to support Anglo's funding requirements beyond the short term.

Around the same time, the Fitch rating agency let it be known that they were going to issue a downgrading for Irish banks generally, and Anglo in particular, and it was believed that the Standard and Poor's rating agency would do something similar. The concern was that this downgrading would lead to an almost automatic reduction in Anglo's liquidity, of the order of several billion euros, since some of Anglo's important corporate depositors would not, as a matter of policy, leave their deposits with a bank which had been downgraded in this manner.

So as work continued on the recapitalisation option for Anglo, and as the deadline for making a capital injection approached, Anglo's situation was deteriorating. Merrill Lynch and NTMA continued to take the view that a nationalised Anglo would be more stable, require less capital and be likely to be able to fund itself in the market. The other key official parties dealing with Anglo, the Department of Finance, the Central Bank and Financial Regulator, were coming around to the same view. In mid-January 2009, after a lengthy discussion, a paper was submitted to the Minister for Finance with a joint recommendation. It said that having regard to the governance issues in Anglo and the continuing liquidity pressures, the Central Bank, Financial Regulator, NTMA, Merrill Lynch and Department of Finance officials were all of the opinion that it was better to nationalise Anglo than to provide it with further capital within the existing structures.

There then followed a little dance. For legal and practical reasons, it was better that Anglo would, in effect, ask to be nationalised as it would help in any dealings with shareholders and other potential claimants. For example, the decision to nationalise could not be presented by them as a Government unreasonably taking away the property rights of shareholders, who would no doubt argue that Anglo might have been saved and that it was Government control which drove it on to the rocks. Much better that the board of Anglo should admit formally in advance that it could not continue without Government help, and that they would voluntarily accept that help in the only form now available – in other words, nationalisation. And so the board of Anglo was advised, with only a relatively short number of hours to go before an expected Extraordinary General Meeting, which had been called so that shareholders could vote to accept a Government capital input, that in fact that capital input was no longer available except in the context of nationalisation: Anglo could in effect go bust, or it could accept the nationalisation option. This gave the board very little room for manoeuvre, and they quickly confirmed – indeed in effect requested – that nationalisation take place.

However, when Donal O'Connor arrived at Government Buildings to indicate formally that the nationalisation 'offer' was accepted, he also brought with him a letter from senior managers of the bank. The execs were clearly taken aback, and their letter expressed a view that all sorts of dire consequences would arise from nationalisation – an early indication that owning this bank was not going to be a trouble-free exercise.

On 15 January, the Minister for Finance announced that Anglo would be nationalised, citing funding difficulties and 'unacceptable practices' that had undermined the reputation of the bank. The legislative provisions for nationalisation that had been drafted during the previous summer and early autumn, and worked on further since, finally were put to the Oireachtas and passed.

7.

NAMA

It was in 2009 that we discovered what an awful thing it is to have to rescue a banking system. First of all, it's not the case that the Government arrives like the heroes on an RNLI lifeboat to drag a sodden but grateful half-drowned wretch out of the perilous ocean to cheers of joy from onlookers on the cliff. It is more like a hard-pressed lifeguard throwing a line to the potential victim to haul him back to the beach, while the crowd on the beach argue about how much line they want to give and the victim argues about how the rescue should be carried out. The victim wants to emerge from the rescue in good physical shape and to carry on his day at the beach with his friends as if nothing has happened. That, after all, is what lifeguards are for.

Rescued banks may, indeed, be grateful – or at least some of their management may be grateful – for help received, but others often continue to act selfishly, without transparency, and in ways which make clear that even though their survival is dependent on the support of the State, which is itself in difficulty, the independent future of their own institution is their priority. Most of the people we dealt with during this period were, like ourselves, doing their best to deal with difficult circumstances. But I came to detest dealing with certain bankers and business people, including one or two who came in as part of management changes after the crisis erupted, who seemed to have no real sense of public responsibility, however good they might be as bank executives.

There were even a few who seemed oblivious to the changes in the fortunes of their institutions. I recall one member of the board of the biggest bank saying indignantly, 'but I am a member of the Court of the Bank of Ireland' in response to some suggestion that his board needed to engage more realistically on some issue or other. I was polite, but I felt like telling him that he was a more like a member of the board of the White Star Line, sitting on the *Titanic* and wondering why the sailors are not saluting properly as they run by in their life vests.

So dealing with the banks on their recapitalisations, on ownership matters, on the terms of the guarantee and so forth – all of this was far from easy going, and with so much at stake it was not always clear who could be trusted to do the right thing and who could not.

What also became clear, very quickly, was how important the guarantee and the support of the Government were to the survival of our banking system. These active and independent institutions developed within a few short weeks a real culture of dependency on the Government, reflecting perhaps how few friends they had left in their private sector relationships.

Many of their day-to-day management problems suddenly seemed incapable of being solved without Government help. Auditors not happy? Send them in to the Department of Finance. Arguing with another bank? Ask the Department or the Central Bank to sort it out. Problems with the Regulator? Ask the NTMA or the Department to intervene. Credit rating agencies not playing ball? Get them to meet the Government. Tax problems in the UK? Call the Department of Finance. And we, as a Department, were increasingly reliant on those of the bank executives who were both professionally capable and engaging positively with the Government.

Most of the people we dealt with retained their sense of professionalism, and many were impressive, skilled individuals, but some seemed to deeply resent the involvement of the Department of Finance in their affairs – only necessary because these banks had to be rescued. Many were not clear on the appropriate relationships of their banks to the various bodies in the State system. More than one bank executive seemed to think that the role of Government officials was to take the blame for the bank's decisions that had not worked out as they would have liked, and some thought that the Department should intervene on their behalf when the regulatory authorities were investigating their behaviour.

It was also in 2009 that the Government decided, in addition to the bank guarantee and the recapitalisations, that there would need to be a further intervention to reduce the overall size of the banking system, and to reduce the impact on the banking system of their most troublesome loan categories, those in relation to property. The basic problem was that, even with the Government showing its willingness to provide capital to the banking system, the market participants who lend to or make deposits with banks – thus making it possible for them to act as banks in the first place – were unsure about the loan books of the banks. They could not be happy that the banks had sufficient capital (and would therefore eventually repay their creditors) while the inherent value of the banks' assets – the loans that they had made – was entirely uncertain. And in Ireland at that point in time there was very little certainty available on that score: the property market was crashing hard; the banks' reputations were heavily damaged; bank managements were not trusted; and the Government was a new player in the banking system, not yet fully known and understood in that role. The market was unlikely to want to lend to banks unless, in addition to capital, they could see a real reduction in the risk levels of the banks.

A standard response to this situation was to put in place a structure to separate out the 'bad' assets and to manage them separately. This kind of asset management structure put in place to isolate risky or poorly performing assets from bank balance sheets is often called a 'bad bank', and it was used in Sweden, Korea and other countries as one way to reduce the risk levels of the banking system. It is, in other words, a fairly typical tool in a banking crisis.

But there is another approach. One can instead provide the banks, for a charge, with a guarantee that their assets will not fall below a particular value. There was in fact a recent model for such a system. In the second half of January 2009, the UK had decided to establish an 'asset protection scheme' along these lines for eligible institutions in that jurisdiction (in the end, I think that only RBS availed of it). In the first few weeks of 2009, we in the Department of Finance and NTMA gave some serious thought to applying a similar tactic to the Irish banks. This approach had two big advantages: there would be no up-front increase in the Irish Government deficit arising from the operation, and no need for the Irish Government to find a lot of funds up-front to finance the scheme. Brendan Mc-Donagh in the NTMA provided the intellectual firepower to analyse this option, with help from NTMA colleagues, including actuary Ronan O'Connor. There were even some very tentative discussions on a 'what-if' basis with some of the banks, because the analysis required access to some of their data.

But among a wide range of pros and cons of this approach, there was one key disadvantage: the process required the Government to take a risk without any proper underwriting of that risk. In other words, we would be selling the banks an insurance policy against losses without knowing what the losses would be in the final analysis. We might rescue the banks, but at what cost? It became clear, relatively quickly, that this uncertainty would be unlikely to be acceptable to the Minister, or to be advocated by his advisors, and that therefore the asset guarantee approach, the insurance approach, was not likely to be put in place.

By contrast to the insurance approach, the asset management or 'bad bank' solution, while it would take longer to implement and would leave the banks in a sort of 'limbo' state for longer than might be comfortable, would make the costs more transparent because each bank would be paid an amount for each loan transferred on the basis of an individual valuation of each asset – a process which should provide greater certainty to the State and to the market.

All of this needed some analysis, and the Minister turned to economist Peter Bacon for that job. Bacon is a well-known and well-regarded economist with extensive experience of working on the property market. He had previously produced two important reports on how the Government should deal with challenges in regard to the burgeoning property market, including the supply and affordability of houses. I had not known him before, but the Minister decided that Bacon was the person for the job and, at the Minister's request, he was appointed as his special adviser at the NTMA (a novel position, created especially for the occasion) for a period of time to allow that work to be carried out. He worked there in co-operation with Brendan McDonagh, John Corrigan and others, reporting regularly also to Michael Somers, the CEO of NTMA, I imagine. At the end of the process, Bacon and the NTMA presented the report in a series of meetings in quick succession.

My recollection is that there was a short preliminary briefing at official level, but the first important presentation was to the Minister, sometime around 20 March 2009. Various senior officials were present: Michael Somers from the NTMA, David Doyle from the Department of Finance, the Governor of the Central Bank, along with a cast of others. Bacon presented his plan, and the various parties listened and responded.

Michael Somers made a key intervention. The State was funded until July, but ongoing funding was not a certainty. It was important that the banking issues were seen to be under control so that markets would continue to provide funds, not just to the banks but to the State. There was no one in the room who did not understand the seriousness of the banking problem, and this intervention underlined it. Big decisions – again – were required, and this was not a surprise.

There was some real concern, though, about the scale of Bacon's plan. He advocated that the State would buy from the banks – at a discount – all the loans that the guaranteed banks had made for 'land and development', mostly speculative activity, and for investment property, which was theoretically less speculative and more likely to provide a real return on the investment. All of this would amount to a face value of the order of €140 to €160 billion, an enormous amount of money.

We all knew that the scale of property lending in Ireland was huge, but Bacon was not advocating taking just the worst performing loans off the banks' balance sheet. His argument was that there was very little faith in the banks' property loan portfolio. If the intention was to help to make the banks viable and fundable again, then they had to be seen to be clean of not just the worst loans, but of all of the loans in the sector which was regarded as most likely to generate losses for the institutions.

This was a strong argument, but the proposed scale of the State's liability in making purchases on this scale would be huge. It might give rise to the very outcome we were trying to avoid – an unwillingness of the markets to fund the State, and therefore the inability of the State to meet its day-to-day obligations and to pay for services. The meeting looked for some compromise that would respect Bacon's suggestion that it was 'bad' categories of loans, not just badly performing loans, that would transfer, while reducing the overall State liability. In the end, it was suggested that there be a modification of the transferrable portfolio to include the whole land and development category and 'associated' investment loans. In other words, where the investment loans were linked on various criteria to loans for land and development purposes, both the land and development loan and the linked investment loan would transfer to the new asset management vehicle – to be called the National Asset Management Agency (NAMA).

Peter Bacon and the NTMA agreed that this approach was viable and credible and it was this modified version of the NAMA proposition that was put to the Taoiseach in a subsequent meeting and then to Government. Many of the same people who had advised the Minister were also present in the meeting with the Taoiseach. The Taoiseach was naturally anxious to ensure that he understood the position of each of the bodies advising him, including external advisers like Merrill Lynch, but also official advisers in the Department of Finance, the NTMA and so forth. As I recall it, he did a full round of the table asking each of the people present to say whether or not they supported this modified NAMA proposition. They all said 'yes', notwithstanding that there was some dissent later, in particular from Michael Somers.

In May 2009, Somers provided a much more negative and pessimistic view of the prospects for NAMA to a meeting of the Oireachtas Public Accounts Committee than he and the NTMA had presented in giving their advice to the Taoiseach and Minister. This puzzled me at the time, and was the subject of at least one lengthy discussion between the Minister and Somers, after which Somers acknowledged that notwithstanding the risks and negative features he saw in NAMA, it was on balance the best option available to Government. But it seems now that Somers never felt convinced by the NAMA idea. He said at the Oireachtas Banking Inquiry that:

> ... the Taoiseach ... asked us all did we support it and I said "Yes." I, kind of, began to get cold feet then about it as time went.... I thought actually, myself, that it would be turned down by the Department of Finance, because the one thing the Department of Finance were very good at was turning down things and I reckoned this would never get past them.[37]

Naturally, I don't agree that the only thing the Department of Finance was good for was turning things down, but it seems clear to me that a very different discussion might have taken place if Michael Somers' concerns were made known at the time the decision was being made. He was, after all, a very capable individual with a high public profile who was leading the institution which had been explicitly asked to provide advice to the Minister on these issues. Insofar as there was banking, financial market and corporate finance expertise available among State employees, it was heavily concentrated in the NTMA and its associated bodies, and NTMA staff were among the key advisers in all of our banking interventions. There was no doubt that Somers' views would have been influential if given in a timely manner.

But, as I am sure Michael Somers would acknowledge, a body like NAMA is a long-term bet that can only be fully judged after years of existence.

In May, 2010 Ambassador Kim, the Korean ambassador to Ireland, kindly invited myself and my wife to dinner at his residence. I knew him a little from previous meetings. He had told me some interesting things about his experience of the Korean financial crisis in the previous decade, during which he was assigned to the Korean embassy in Paris. It was a small dinner, just a few guests, including some Dublin-based Korean business people. His residence was on the south side, so I got lost, had to make an embarrassed phone call for directions and therefore turned up quite a few minutes late – a *faux pas* that seemed to be overlooked, and instead it was good-naturedly noted by the Korean guests that we had arrived in my Hyundai i30, a good Korean car.

Apart from the courtesy element of the invitation, I wondered if the ambassador had some particular purpose in inviting us, and indeed during the course of the evening he passed me an envelope which I opened immediately. Inside there was a copy of the annual report of the Korean version of NAMA. By then it was more than a decade old, having been instituted to deal with the fallout of the Asian crisis in 1997. It had been, in terms of assets transferred from the banking system, not dissimilar to the size of our NAMA, and had applied discounts to the transferred assets which were also not dissimilar to the NAMA experience (around 65 per cent in the Korean case). And after all these years it seemed they had not just recovered their costs but were left with a few billion dollars' worth of assets yet to sell. In cash terms they would be making a profit at the end. I already knew a little about the Korean experience, but NAMA was barely off the ground, and it was nice to see that in another place and in other circumstances, a NAMA-like structure had done its business and was working out okay in the end – but the project most definitely must be seen as a long-term one.

NAMA has been controversial, and we often associate controversy with failures. But it was expected to be controversial. With billions of euros of public monies at stake, with reputations and careers and financial futures of individuals on the line, with thousands of loan contracts and many millions of pages of documentation involved, and with enormous political stakes as well, it could hardly avoid being controversial. So if the NAMA chairman and chief executive are in the newspaper headlines more than is usual for the leaders of even a major State agency, this is not a failing but almost a design feature of the structure. As I said in my statement to the Oireachtas Banking Inquiry:

> ... it was always envisaged that this structure ... would almost certainly be controversial at all stages of its life ... it would be amazing if there were not a multitude of voices pressing one agenda or another, in the media or in the courts. That NAMA's work should be controversial ... is no sign of failure.

Some of the controversy was natural, even necessary, but much of the comment was ill-informed or contradictory. In 2012 Brendan McDonagh was moved to publish an article[38] entitled 'Busting NAMA Myths', in which he said:

> The agency has been accused of many things – many of them conflicting and often by the same voices who

have no difficulty expressing contradictory positions. Initially, it was that NAMA would pay the banks too much for loans; then it became that NAMA has not paid enough for the loans; that NAMA is soft on developers; that NAMA is pursuing developers too aggressively; that NAMA should have a social remit; that NAMA should only have a commercial remit.

Nowadays, NAMA is well established and is in the news, it seems, just about every day. But in the Spring of 2009, it was still just a concept that might not get off the ground. There were two important pre-conditions for the establishment of NAMA. The first but less important one was that when loans were transferred to NAMA, the borrowings to fund these loan purchases would not be classified as part of the Irish Government's debt, on the basis of the EU standard statistical rules. If they were so classified, Ireland's apparent debt when looked at in all the key international tables would be much higher than the real underlying debt of the Government. At the same time, various vehicles created to assist banks in other European states were being classified in a way which did not affect apparent Government debt, and a different treatment for Ireland would make us look bad by comparison. Of course, this is just a matter of optics, but in the world of markets, optics matter. We did not wish to hide what we were doing, but we did want it to be accounted for in a favourable way.

The second and bigger issue was where to find the cash that NAMA would need to operate properly. The way it was supposed to work was that NAMA – acting in effect for the Irish Government – would buy loans previously made by the banks, and would pay the banks for these loans but at a discount to the value of the loans on the banks' books. Thus borrowers would now owe the same amount of money to NAMA as they had owed to the bank concerned, on the same terms. But NAMA would pay less to the bank concerned than the original loan amount. The banks would take a loss, or at least would have to recognise the loss already inherent in the loan. Those losses would lead in turn to an increase in the capital the banks would require to offset the losses. However, the banks would at a stroke be smaller and more stable institutions. Better still, the funds received in payment for the transferred loans would boost their weak liquidity position. The problem was that if the Irish State tried to borrow tens of billions of euros in a short time period to pay for these loans from the banks, there was a significant probability that it would not be able to do so at a reasonable interest rate. The cash would have to come from somewhere else.

To deal with the accounting/statistical issues, Brendan McDonagh and I got together with an expert from the Central Statistics Office who was able to explain in detail how the EU rules would treat NAMA. It seemed clear that NAMA would not achieve the favourable treatment we wanted.

We argued a little with the statistician. The rules did not seem to us to treat bodies with a similar purpose in different countries in exactly the same way. And yet, these were the rules we were dealing with. The CSO – an independent statistical agency with its own obligations – could not magically make them go away and must act within the rules as they exist. The rules would not be broken. Eventually, I drew a few boxes on a scrap of paper to represent a particular but quite strange corporate structure. McDonagh built on that and drew a few boxes of his own. If the statistical rules must be followed to the letter, could NAMA be structured in this way to achieve the more favourable classification? It looked more promising.

We were on to something: there was a chance we could solve the statistical problem.

The solution needed to be much more refined, but the discussion that day was the first step to developing the final, rather artificial corporate structure of NAMA. In effect, at the bottom of the NAMA corporate structure is a body whose debts are not classified as part of overall Government debt because it is majority-owned by non-government entities who made a relatively small investment and are guaranteed a commercial return on it. So we have ended up with a structure which is intended to serve the public interest, the vast bulk of whose risks and returns are borne by the State, but in which the State is formally only a minority shareholder. The practical implications of this – beyond some technical inconveniences – were not expected to be great, but the difference it makes to the accounting/statistical treatment is quite significant. Of course, statistical rules change over time, and it seems to me to be unlikely that the same structure would pass muster if a similar circumstance were to arise in the future.

The scraps of paper that formed the basis of the NAMA corporate structure are still somewhere in Department of Finance files, and they now look like little more than a few meaningless doodles.

More important than the statistical problem was how to find the cash to give to the banks as the consideration for the loans that they transferred to NAMA. Since we were dealing with banks, the banks could in theory lend NAMA the money that it would then hand back to them as payment. Or more precisely, NAMA would pay the banks by issuing bonds to them. While this would transfer the ownership and risk of the loans to NAMA, leaving the banks with much less risky NAMA bonds, backed by the Irish State, it would not generate any cash for the cash-strapped Irish banks, reducing the benefit of the NAMA structure.

The solution to this problem was relatively simple: let the banks bring the NAMA bonds to the European Central Bank and use them as collateral to borrow cash from the ECB. The ECB would not be lending to the Government – which is entirely prohibited – but in a roundabout way it would be providing the cash to finance the NAMA transactions. Simple. But simple only so long as the ECB did not object to being the indirect financier for tens of billions of euros in Irish loan transfers.

In developing the NAMA proposal in this way, we could have trusted to our own interpretation of ECB rules, and hoped that they would not change, but it seemed much safer to engage with the ECB properly. A delegation was sent to Frankfurt. John Hurley and Michael Somers explained the proposed structure to Mr Trichet, President of the ECB. At the same time, myself, Tony Grimes of the Central Bank and John Corrigan from NTMA met, as I recall, Gonzalez-Paramo from the Executive Board of the ECB, who was accompanied by a number of colleagues including John Fell, a senior staff member, who later became an important part of many of the Troika delegations to Ireland. The ECB was very helpful indeed. So long as the NAMA bonds transferred to the banks were designed in such a way as to meet the collateral standards of the ECB, the Irish banks could borrow from the ECB on the strength of them. Without this assurance the NAMA project might have been still-born, and we greatly appreciated the ECB's help at the time.

The Government's initial decision on the NAMA initiative was taken in early April 2009, but the complexities of the legislative drafting, the practical preparations required and the level of genuine political concern and opposition involved all meant that NAMA itself was not legally established until November of that year, and only then could the lengthy process of valuing and transferring loans from the banks formally start.

In the meanwhile, practical arrangements for NAMA were put in train. The NTMA, through letters from Minister Lenihan to its CEO, was required to make the necessary support available to the interim managing director of NAMA and to the advisory board that was being established to prepare the way for the new agency. Brendan McDonagh was Lenihan's and the Government's natural choice for the interim MD post given his work on developing the project, and later became CEO of the new agency. Frank Daly, formerly Ireland's top tax collector as Chairman of the Revenue Commissioners, was appointed a few months later to chair the board of NAMA on its formal establishment in December 2009.

While all of the practical and legislative preparations for NAMA were put in place, other elements of the ongoing bank rescue continued as recapitalisation costs mounted (slowly in 2009 compared to the following year).

NAMA was a very difficult 'sell' for the Government parties, and there were many internal voices who quite naturally worried about the scale of it and the potential for it to go seriously wrong. In the Green Party, as the smaller coalition partner with long-term concerns about Irish planning and spatial development very close to their hearts, there seemed to be a particular need to keep party activists on board, and John Gormley and Eamon Ryan had to put their personal reputations on the line to keep the project afloat with their party constituency. Ryan had been assigned the difficult task of tracking the development of the financial crisis on behalf of the Greens, developing their party viewpoint and representing it within the Government system. He was naturally in regular contact with Minister Lenihan, and less often with myself, but he was very steady under pressure. Around the time that the NAMA proposal was being brought to Government for decision he met myself and David Doyle on the way to a meeting. His message was not to find a compromise between all the conflicting demands that would certainly inform the NAMA debate, but that if this particular job needs to be done, then be sure to do it right.

There were quite a few personnel changes among people dealing with the banking crisis in the latter part of 2009 and the first few weeks of 2010. Patrick Honohan took over in September 2009 from John Hurley as Governor of the Central Bank. Hurley had been asked to extend his previous term as Governor, which had finished in March 2009, and while in theory his extension had been for seven years it was always Hurley's intention that he would stay only for a few months.

One of Hurley's last acts was the search for a new CEO of the Financial Regulator, a process finalised by his successor, Patrick Honohan. In October, Honohan announced the proposed appointment of Matthew Elderfield to the post, to take effect in January 2010. He took over from Mary O'Dea, former head of consumer protection issues in the Financial Regulator who had been acting on an interim basis since the retirement of Pat Neary early in the year.

Eugene Sheehy also stepped down in the autumn of 2009 as CEO of AIB – a move which had been announced earlier in the year. AIB chairman Dan O'Connor (who had taken over from Dermot Gleeson in April) took on the role of executive chairman pending a replacement for Sheehy. In December, Michael Somers retired from the NTMA and was replaced by John Corrigan, reflecting John's involvement in managing the banking crisis up to then. Not long after John's arrival the split of responsibilities between the NTMA and the Department of Finance was put on a more formal footing, but the working relationship continued to be close.

In the Department of Finance, too, there was some change. After the retirement of David Doyle, the Government appointed me as Secretary General. I got the news from Minister Lenihan, who called me down to his office, where David Doyle was already present. The Minister had me sit on the little sofa in his office and quite ceremoniously gave me the good news. It was a great honour for me, but I must not have displayed the expected demeanour because the Minister wondered aloud why I did not appear delighted. It was indeed an honour, and the pinnacle of any Irish civil service career, but it was clear that it was not going to be a pleasant tour of duty. So much had gone wrong in our economic system, and so much more was still going wrong that, while I was pleased to get the job, there was not much cause for joy.

8.

Lenihan as Minister

One of the principles that defined the Irish civil service during my career in it was political impartiality – civil servants were there to serve whichever Government had been elected and there were various rules in place to prevent any but the more junior grades from being active in party politics. While no group is more interested in politics than civil servants, other than maybe the politicians themselves, generally speaking any political affiliations are closely guarded. Discussing party preferences at work was something that was – for the vast bulk of civil servants – rarely done. I could count on my fingers the number of civil servants I have dealt with over the years whose party preferences I would know. For my part, I have worked with politicians and their politically oriented special advisers from at least five parties over the years, and have never let their parties determine my advice.

But political impartiality does not lead one to be blind to the strengths and weaknesses of one's political bosses. During the financial crisis the extreme stresses brought out some examples of selfishness, hypocrisy and unpleasantness among leading politicians and public servants, but others of real moral, political or even physical courage and perseverance. There were many people whose response to the crisis was unselfish commitment to first stemming, and then seeking to repair, the terrible damage done. An example was Brian Lenihan.

I found out about Brian Lenihan's cancer diagnosis at the same time as everybody else, when the news was broadcast by Ursula Halligan, then with the TV3 station, in December 2009. By then I had been working closely with him for more than a year and a half and, despite occasional mutual frustrations, had come to know and like him enough that this news was something of a blow – how much more difficult, then, for his family and friends.

Naturally, since we were in the middle of a very difficult financial crisis, my colleagues and I were also very concerned about how this illness might impact on the management of the Department of Finance and of the country. The soon-to-retire Secretary General of the Department, David Doyle, was practical and compassionate at this moment. Hand sanitisation stations appeared around the Department and especially in the passage to the Minister's office, and staff were told to be sure to use them to minimise any danger of infection to the Minister. A reclining chair was brought into the Minister's office so that he could rest when he needed to. Senior managers were told to reduce the length and number of meetings with the Minister. The Minister's private secretary, Dermot Moylan, who managed his office and much of his workflow, was given the impossible task of maintaining some control over the Minister's natural inclination to expand his working day rather than reduce it.

In fact, in my opinion, Lenihan became a somewhat better Minister after his diagnosis. To me, he seemed more focussed, he conducted his business more efficiently by prioritising more, he reduced his external appointments and so had less distraction. But he was the Minister for Finance in an economic crisis. The simple fact is that one cannot hold that position and yet be only partially engaged. Despite our efforts to reduce his work to the essentials, it was never possible to reduce the huge pressures on Lenihan to the level appropriate to a person with such a serious illness, and there were moments when he had to work or travel when it was clear that he ought to be resting.

Even though I was appointed by the Government as Secretary General of the Department of Finance only a few weeks after his diagnosis, Lenihan and I did not speak in depth very often about his illness, though it hovered in the background of many conversations. Of necessity, we talked occasionally about his treatment and the impact that it would have on his work. At various points in his therapy it was clear that there would be moments when he would be more drained and require more rest than at others, and we would work around those to the extent that we could. Sometimes, though, drained or not, he simply had to engage with important matters that could not wait. Officials can do as much as possible to reduce a Minister's workload, but they simply don't have the democratic mandate to take on the role of a Minister in his stead.

Naturally enough, after I was appointed as Secretary General of the Department of Finance, I had received some low-key messages from the Taoiseach's staff that the Taoiseach would like me to be sensitive to the Minister's situation, and of course to report to him (the Taoiseach) if it seemed to me that the illness was reaching a point where he could not function properly. And from time to time I would be called over to the Taoiseach to give him my update on the economic and banking issues we were facing, separately from the regular briefings he was getting from Lenihan. Of course, Lenihan knew and approved of this – I kept him informed – and he would have wanted the same himself had he been Taoiseach.

I was not surprised, but wondered about the wisdom of it, when Lenihan told me toward the end of 2010 or early 2011 that he had decided to run again for the Dáil. It was clear that his illness would mean he would not – or at least perhaps ought not – take a leading role in politics after the election. But Lenihan told me that his medical advice was that perhaps it was good to stay actively involved, even if not in a leadership position.

After the election, though, when he had won his seat as the only remaining Fianna Fáil deputy elected in Dublin, there was a short period before the new Government took office during which Lenihan remained Finance Minister on a care-taking basis. During that time he told me (more than once, so I know it was playing on his mind somewhat) how important it was to him that his constituency had returned him again to the Dáil, and in particular that his family could take some real comfort from the fact that his contribution as a Minister had been vindicated by his own electorate.

Lenihan was an unusual person. Like anyone, at moments he was not easy to get along with, but much more usually he was polite and friendly. His mind worked overtime so the tele-phone might ring late at night or early in the morning if he had some new information to digest or some idea that he wanted to talk through. Indeed, his way of thinking about an issue was often to talk about it from a range of different angles, first taking one line, then another, until his opinion was formed. Sometimes in a moment of thoughtlessness or frustration he would make comments that were more cutting than he intend-ed, and in those cases there was usually an immediate apology or a more generous assessment of whatever had generated the first impatient remark.

I think he aimed, consciously, to be humble. A leading US financier coming to Dublin asked for a meeting with Lenihan, who readily agreed since, of course, this was a time when potential investors were always welcome. In the course of an introductory discussion this gentleman dropped quite a few names including that of George W. Bush, whom he indicated he knew, but whose merits and intellect, he opined, left a great deal to be deserved. But if that was the case, Lenihan wondered, how had Bush managed to be elected as the US President? 'Just because he had the same name as his famous father,' was the answer. Lenihan did not bristle, or explain that he was himself the namesake of his own famous father, a long-serving Minister in previous Irish Governments. He simply said, 'that can happen all right'.

He was proud of his own erudition. After a very serious conversation with Christine Lagarde, then French Finance Minister and now the managing director of the IMF, he recounted to me the details of the conversation but made sure to remind me that 'of course, I spoke to her in French'. But, in the moments of calm which did present themselves over the course of a tumultuous few years, his breadth of both education and interest were surprising. A simple remark from me on some past event might generate a detailed history of some Irish locale, or of how some minor point of law had developed and become crucial to a historical event. I even recall, while we were sharing a flight back from a meeting abroad, his giving me a small lecture on the optics of a 'Brocken Spectre' – a magnificently sharp and clear shadow image of our aircraft projected onto a cloud bank on our right, by the sunlight above and to the left of us, and surrounded by a clearly delineated rainbow-like spectrum of light that formed a perfect circle around the aircraft's shadow.

In the last few months of Lenihan's time as Minister his illness seemed to be changing him physically. He was more gaunt, his face a touch hollowed, his skin more sallow. On one occasion around this time he summoned some journalists who had been waiting outside the Department's offices into our conference room for an update on some situation or other – an impromptu press conference which I would have advised against, had I had the chance. He looked ill and tired, and I grabbed hold of Eoin Dorgan, his press officer at the time, subsequently an adviser to Michael Noonan. I told Eoin that Lenihan should not do this press conference looking as he did – it would certainly be commented on, I said, and the Minister might regret it. What can be done? Eoin informed me that he had a bottle of Touche Éclat, some kind of cover-all makeup which the Minister might be persuaded to use before facing the photographers. There was then a moment of unspoken communication between us, as I think we each pondered what turn in our careers had led us to a professional discussion on the merits of Touche Éclat.

It would be easy, of course, to catalogue Lenihan's minor faults and foibles, but there seems little point in that, and I will leave it to others to assess his term as Minister. To me, the key question in assessing him as a person is how, when confronted with enormous national decisions to make and great personal stress arising from his work and his illness, did he respond. The answer to that is courageously, and with dignity.

9.

Trichet's Worries

During the first half of 2010, the intensive pace of work in dealing with the banking crisis continued, but each new intervention to support the banks added to the pressure on the State's overall debt position. NAMA started the process of transferring assets from the banks in three tranches, starting with the biggest individual exposures, but each successive transfer to NAMA would lead to the realisation of losses in the banks, and therefore to a need for Government to recapitalise them. And the NAMA losses were turning out to be far worse than expected – the final overall discount was 57 per cent. In other words, the loans were turning out to be worth less than half of their face value, based on the NAMA valuation process. Worse, the valuation and transfer process was a drawn out one, and because the discounts on the first tranche were considerably larger than expected (in large part because the quality of the loans made by the banks were worse than expected), it was not possible to provide reassurance to the market that the eventual final discount levels would be manageable for the State in terms of the bank recapitalisations required. The new information about loan quality that was emerging from NAMA, together with ongoing very poor economic conditions and the continuing collapse of the property market, meant that meeting the capital requirements of the banks was increasingly looking like trying to hit a moving target.

The Central Bank, now led by Honohan and Elderfield, made a strong attempt to get to the bottom of the capital requirements of the main banks, excluding Anglo which was to be treated separately. Results of a rigorous stress test were published in the spring, after a major technical effort by the Central Bank system. These stress tests took account of NAMA valuations as far as they were known at that stage, and also the expected scenario for the economy, while allowing for the risk of some worsening of that scenario.

Finally, there seemed to be a moment of respite. Commentators responded well to the stress test results. They seemed credible and market participants thought that they might finally rely on these Central Bank figures, even if discounts on future transfers from the banks to NAMA were difficult to predict. Bank of Ireland, in a slightly better state than the other big banks, managed to raise some new funds from the private sector after the announcement of the Central Bank stress tests that spring, perhaps the first real sign of positive movement in two years. Maybe after many months of struggling against the momentum of a fast moving crisis, we were starting to get some purchase.

But we could not catch a break. Just at the moment when we were trying to bottom out the Irish banking problem, the Greek state entered into its sovereign debt crisis, with contagion effects for the rest of Europe. The first Greek bailout took place in May 2010, but did little to assuage growing concerns in markets about sovereign risks in other European countries, including Ireland. It became clear over the summer that investor sentiment regarding both the Irish State and Irish banks was worsening yet again. In the Department of Finance I was advising a temporarily reluctant Brian Lenihan that both the banking interventions and the fiscal adjustments were going to have to be larger than we had planned up to then.

If it were not for the fast deteriorating international situation, the banking announcements made by Lenihan and the Central Bank in September 2010 might have had a more positive effect than they did. The spring stress test results had been intended to expose the depths of the problems in the Irish banks, and had been reasonably well received, but they had not dealt with the worst case – Anglo – and the horrendous level of potential losses in that institution were still not fully quantified. Moreover, the continued work on transferring bank assets to NAMA was exposing losses at a greater level than had been pencilled in for the purposes of the stress tests. And as the government injected cash into the banks to make up for their losses it was taking an increasingly large ownership stake in each of them, until eventually all but Bank of Ireland were effectively in State ownership, and even Bank of Ireland was a close call in that regard.

Now, in the September 2010 announcements, the Government and the Central Bank were trying to restore credibility to the official position – recapitalisations would now take account both of the additional NAMA losses and of the expected losses in Anglo (though not on a 'worst case' basis). Subordinated bondholders in Anglo would be expected to share some of these costs by taking a loss on their bonds, but senior bondholders would be left untouched, it was said. Moreover, the Government would remain committed to a strong plan of fiscal adjustment and would publish a four-year economic plan in the coming months to underpin that.

Some commentators were impressed by the announcements and the resolve of the Government. Ireland continued to be willing to make the kind of large commitments that were required to get ahead of the huge banking problem.

But any positive sentiment was short-lived. There was just too much bad news, domestically and internationally. Bond investors were increasingly risk-averse, and the ever increasing debt of the Irish State, driven by both the ongoing fiscal problems and the growing bank rescue burden, combined in their minds with the risks of disruption among all the euro area peripheral economies. In that context, Ireland was just not seen as a good investment, whether in relation to the banks or the sovereign State.

So it was perhaps no surprise that the Minister would get a concerned telephone call from Mr Trichet, President of the ECB.

Trichet's call

It was, to the best of my recollection, a Thursday or Friday in the latter part of September 2010. Brian Lenihan took a call from Jean-Claude Trichet. I was in the room with Lenihan, or perhaps was called down to his office when Trichet's call came in. I could hear only Lenihan's side of the conversation but Trichet was apparently in full flight, demanding to know what Ireland was doing about the continuing pressure on the fiscal and banking position. Lenihan and I were a bit puzzled. Trichet – or at least the ECB – was well informed and knew that Ireland continued to make huge efforts to get the economic position under control, though not helped by mixed messages from Europe and the terrible turnaround in investor sentiment that engulfed Greece and was now infecting other sovereign borrowers. Indeed, earlier that year, Trichet had called Irish action 'courageous and convincing'.[39] But that was then, and Trichet knew that the cost of banking rescues was mounting and that the banking system was ever more indebted to the ECB. But what more did he want us to do? That was not at all clear.

Lenihan explained the actions that were under way. Bringing transparency to the banking losses and restructuring the banking system were a priority, a new four year plan was being developed to be published in November, to be followed by a Budget for 2011 which Lenihan was already publicly saying would be a lot harsher than had been predicted before the summer. Every reasonable action was being taken but big and apparently intractable problems remained.

Trichet demanded that the European Commission be allowed to come to Ireland to examine the situation – an immediate mission from the Commission was required, he said. Lenihan covered the phone briefly to ask me about that. I explained the request was a bit redundant, since a Commission team would in fact be in town (from recollection, as soon as the following Tuesday) precisely for the purpose of getting a better insight into events in Ireland. Lenihan said this to Trichet, who told Lenihan this was not good enough – why could they not come immediately? Lenihan said they can come whenever they want, of course, but Tuesday was not a long time away. Perhaps Trichet had made an equally impassioned call to Ollie Rehn at the European Commission, because we heard almost immediately that the Commission mission was being brought forward – by one day.

When the team arrived, their work had a somewhat confused start. They had not been in touch with us to tell us their precise agenda – which had probably been overturned by the Trichet intervention – and when I asked them where they wanted to start they were not really sure. Clearly, the instructions to advance their meeting had not come with any precision as to the programme of work they were to follow. But it was clear enough to both sides the range of topics that ought to be covered over the course of their visit, and we had staff members from each of the relevant divisions of the Department on standby, so one of my colleagues was despatched to set up a series of presentations from Department of Finance staff over the course of that day. In the meanwhile I took the visiting mission to an establishment a few yards away to keep them in chat for half an hour while we got set up, and to try to get to know these people who might well be more regular visitors in the coming months.

The team was led by Istvan Szekely, formerly an IMF official now working in the Commission, and only just assigned to responsibility for Irish economic matters within the Commission's Economic and Finance Directorate General (known as DG-ECFIN). He was a Hungarian econometrician[40] and when I had a chance to speak to him privately he outlined some concerns he had. He thought our growth expectations were too high, based on econometric approaches which took more account of scarce credit conditions. He was also concerned that if the economy performed less well than expected, we could overshoot our deficit targets. We also discussed the dangers to access to sovereign credit markets, and almost *sotto voce* he noted that while it was not the purpose of his mission, he would be expected to make an initial precautionary assessment of the potential for an EU/IMF programme in his reports back to his bosses in the Commission (to include, I supposed, Ollie Rehn, the Commissioner and Marco Buti, the Director General of the relevant part of the Commission). So this mission, pre-planned and whose principal purpose was entirely different, nonetheless became an early opportunity for the potential parties to a negotiation to meet each other at a technical level.

Somehow, however, this short opening mission, or an earlier meeting with ECB officials, managed to get exaggerated in subsequent media commentary with suggestions that there was a permanent team of ECB advisors operating in the Department of Finance from September 2010.

Even if there was no 'permanent team', there were considerably more contacts between Irish authorities and the European Commission, ECB and IMF than in a typical year, reflecting the difficulty of Ireland's position and also the implications for the broader European system. In addition to a range of more 'normal' contacts with the Commission and other institutions, there was a series of additional discussions throughout the autumn. For example, in September there was an evening meeting in Brussels, with Olli Rehn representing the Commission and Jürgen Stark the ECB. On 19/20 October there was a meeting at official level in Brussels. There was a detailed meeting between Rehn, Stark and Lenihan, with accompanying officials, on 25 October to hammer out an agreement on the fiscal tightening to be expected over the following years. On 8 November, Olli Rehn came to Dublin. There were various other contacts in the meantime, and finally, on the weekend when two Ministers said there were no negotiations ongoing on a bailout, a group of 15 or so Irish officials flew out to Brussels for a two-day sequence of meetings on Sunday and Monday, 14–15 November 2010, with a similarly large group of IMF, ECB and European Commission officials in Brussels. More about all of these below.

10.

Back and Forth with Brussels

On 22 September, a small team accompanied Minister Lenihan to Brussels for what was to be a confidential discussion. It included myself, Jim O'Brien, Ann Nolan, Alan Ahearne, Michael McGrath and Cathy Herbert. We got out of two cars in the parking basement underneath the famous Berlaymont Building in Brussels, which housed the offices of the various Commissioners, where we were met by someone from Commissioner Olli Rehn's office. We were shown into a lift, and from there to a long corridor, and to the door of a dining room where some of the team were asked to remain outside and the rest were asked to be seated. This was the first time I had ever been to such a meeting in the Commission – we were clearly in enough trouble to merit this special treatment. I remember looking at the menu on the table in front of me and thinking 'humble pie'.

The discussion was being hosted by Olli Rehn, who as the Commissioner in charge of DG-ECFIN was the closest thing that the EU had to a Finance Minister. Rehn had an open and friendly personality, and would be no one's pushover, but he was not doctrinaire and wanted to address and solve problems. Over the years that we dealt with him, he was regarded rightly as a good European and a friend to Ireland. After his high-profile years as European Commissioner, he was elected to the European Parliament, but very shortly afterwards returned to Finland to serve as a Minister in the Finnish Government.

His most senior civil servant, the very experienced Director General Marco Buti, was also present, with some others. Most of my experience in European matters was with people dealing with financial services legislation, or taxation, so I did not know Buti at this point, but I had had complimentary reports from Jim O'Brien, who was Ireland's representative on the European Economic and Financial Committee, and who therefore knew some of the DG-ECFIN people quite well.

Jürgen Stark, one of the Executive Board members of the European Central Bank,[41] and one of the six most senior ECB managers, as well as a member of the Governing Council which makes all the big policy decisions, was also present. His duties within the ECB were such that he was often referred to as its 'Chief Economist'. He exhibited a strong belief that early and aggressive fiscal adjustment would be important in overcoming Irish economic problems, but he had a pragmatic side which we discovered later.

The discussion over dinner quickly settled into what was becoming a familiar pattern: a recap of recent events, a run over the current political considerations, a restatement of the very real efforts Ireland was making to correct its position, gentle (in the circumstances) pressure from the Commission to consider how we would react if fiscal pressures worsened, and a very clear and distinct demand for greater effort from the ECB. But there was not a conclusion, and at this stage no one present was openly advocating a bailout loan package from the EU and IMF – in fact, most of those present would prefer to avoid it, I felt at the time.

Perhaps, this being a confidential meeting, no one had told the building services that there would be people in that part of the building until late. So about the time we exited the dining room to re-join our colleagues outside, all the lights in the corridors went dark. Lenihan held back for a private discussion with Rehn. Lenihan told me later that Rehn thought it was still more likely than not that a bailout could be avoided – though it had to be considered a possibility – even, according to Lenihan, implying that the Portuguese were a more likely candidate for bailout at that stage than Ireland. Perhaps Lenihan was reading too much between the lines on that.

But outside, where a group of us were mingling while waiting in the dark for our bosses to conclude, Marco Buti told me that it was his personal view that a bailout for Ireland would on balance probably be required. He was not advocating it, at this stage, merely giving an opinion on the likely turn of events. He wanted us to be prepared, and he was clear that the Commission would be preparing too. So, even if neither the European nor the Irish political systems were yet prepared for an Irish bailout, it could certainly be seen as featuring in the thoughts of European policy makers, at least on a precautionary basis, as the most likely 'Plan B' from then on.

For Ireland, however, it was considered too soon to contemplate it. First, an EU/IMF bailout would provide funding for the Government, not for the banks. At the time, the Government had plenty of cash, having made a conscious effort through the NTMA to beef up cash balances. And although the yields on Irish Government paper were getting much too high for comfort, the last NTMA bond auction had actually gone alright – the target amount had been raised.

Worryingly, however, there was plenty of speculation about an Irish 'need' for a bailout, and this kind of talk could easily become a self-fulfilling prophecy. When the IMF lends money to a country, it requires that it take priority over other creditors. Why does this matter? Well, if I am about to lend to Ireland, I would normally expect to be paid on the same basis as other creditors. So if Country A owes €100 billion, and can only pay back €75 billion, I would expect to get paid back three-quarters of my loan. On the other hand, if half of that €100 billion comes from the IMF, the IMF takes the first €50 billion and the rest of the creditors, who are owed €50 billion in total, have to settle for the remaining €25 billion – they get only half. The presence of the IMF in the mix has devalued the other loans, and for a time at least the private sector is less willing to make a loan to Country A.

Moreover, if there is increasing speculation about an IMF bailout of Country A, the potential private sector lenders will be concerned that there is information about Country A that they do not have – in other words, that the prospects for Country A are worsening, and thus the probability of a default may appear to have increased.

So for the investor, a key measure of risk is the probability of a default on their loan and the likely size of the loss in the event of a default. And apparently credible speculation about IMF involvement changes the investors' view of each of these numbers, making it less likely they will want to lend, closing down the access that the country concerned has to the market, and increasing the interest rate that the country has to pay to borrow. At a certain point, the increased interest rate becomes unsustainable – the country cannot be expected to be able to pay that interest rate on a large portion of its debt, and when investors believe that point has been reached, they will simply cease to lend to the country concerned at almost any reasonable interest rate.

The irony, therefore, is that the availability of a rescue for a country in trouble can accelerate the need for one. For that reason, no Irish official would be likely to speculate in public on an IMF bailout. But lots of other people seemed to think they could speak on Ireland's behalf, or to make their own guesses seem like fact, in briefings and 'leaks' to newspapers and others. So there were regular denials or rebuttals of one story or another suggesting that there was any Irish Government plan to seek a bailout.

But if a bailout were to be avoided, Irish efforts to convince markets that investors should continue to buy Irish government bonds had to be successful, and the signs on this were not good.

During September, a real effort had been made to get to the bottom of the problem of Anglo-Irish Bank. Anglo's situation had continued to worsen, in particular because the expected discounts on NAMA purchases of its loan book were turning out to be much worse than had originally been expected. Of course, property prices had been continually worsening which meant additional losses on Anglo's loans to property developers. In the absence of any willing buyers it was hard to say what the value of any asset would be. Moreover, there was a real problem that the assets that NAMA was purchasing in the banking market were not turning out to have the characteristics that NAMA had been led to expect – on various measures, the loans were not as good as they should have been. All of this was reflected in NAMA's payment of a lower price for the assets than might have been expected, thus leading to greater losses and a greater capital need for the banks.

The announcement of a 'definitive' indication of the losses in Anglo at end-September 2010, accompanied by a need for additional capital for AIB, created some stir in the market, and was met with mixed reviews. Some commentators were happier with a big number which might be seen as getting all the remaining bad news out at once, and allowing a firmer platform for policy thereafter. Others worried that the newly announced losses, which would add to the Irish national debt, would not be easily managed in the midst of what was a fast developing sovereign debt crisis. Since the previous May, led by the difficulties in Greece, markets were taking increasingly sceptical views of a number of countries and were less and less willing to lend to them. Interest rates on their bonds had to rise to provide a sufficient reward to tempt investors to invest in these countries' 'risky' sovereign bonds. For Ireland, this trend had continued throughout September, and towards the end of the month the cost of borrowing reached the point that, in tandem with the announcement on the capital requirements of Anglo, the Government stated that it would not borrow any further funds for a period, and in the meanwhile would draw down on the large cash pile it held precisely for this type of eventuality.

There is no particular 'magic number' level at which interest rates become unsustainably high for a sovereign borrower – it depends on all sorts of factors. But some commentators had decided that a 7 per cent yield might be seen as a 'cut-off' point, after which a country should be seen as being in trouble. Irish yields were heading for that point. On 28 September David McWilliams posted this on his Twitter account: 'Irish bond yields touching 7 per cent, 6.99 per cent actually. Once they break 7, its curtains.' Some of my colleagues interpreted that comment as being a bit too gleeful for comfort, but there was at least reason to hope that the announcements to be made the next day on the banking outlook would be sufficiently realistic to convince the markets that the costs were still manageable.

In fact, as mentioned above, market reaction to the banking announcements were initially neutral to positive, with a real fall-off in interest rates on Irish bonds. But there was no great sigh of relief – the debt burden might now be better estimated, but it was still very high (and would be higher still later) and in the context of a very negative trend for European periphery bonds, there was only short-term relief. For a while, the negative trend ameliorated, and by mid-October the interest rate on an Irish ten-year bond was around 6.2 per cent. This reduction in bond interest rates may have been the result of activity by the ECB in bond markets, but it was despite the fact that rating agencies Moody's and DBRS announced they were considering a downgrade of Ireland.

Banking outflows continued, however, and the ECB concerns that had led to the phone call from Trichet to Lenihan in September had not abated. Indeed, as many of the bonds issued by Irish banks under the original guarantee programme (now replaced by a second version) matured in September 2010, the overall reliance of the Irish banking system on central bank funding had increased considerably. This was inevitable, and expected, but combined with the pattern of outflows, it left the ECB anxious and even angry. They wanted Ireland to have a 'Plan B', but the only one available seemed to be to seek assistance from the IMF and EU partners, which would not directly address bank liquidity. An alternative, or indeed complementary, approach might be a much bigger frontloading of fiscal adjustments – in other words, a large set of cutbacks in Budget 2010. But this would risk further slowdown in the economy. The major adjustments already made had been more or less accepted by the public, but the consequences, economic and political, of further large adjustments in the coming year were not clear.

Back to Brussels

It was against this background that Lenihan, myself, Michael McGrath and others flew out to Brussels on 25 October 2010 to see European Commissioner Olli Rehn and ECB Executive Board Member Jürgen Stark.

This meeting was again in the Commission premises in the Berlaymont Building in Brussels, though it looked and felt different in the brightness of daytime. The building is modern and well-kept (and had quite recently emerged from a years-long fundamental refurbishment prompted, I think, by the need to modernise and clear asbestos from the building). The meeting rooms are quite ordinary. They don't convey any particular sense of history or occasion, and the tables are narrow enough that there is no artificial distance between opposite sides – ideal for a simple technical discussion, albeit at a relatively high level.

The first part of the meeting was with the European Commission only, maintaining for a brief moment the fiction that the ECB was present to deal mostly with banking matters. Rehn greeted us with his usual courtesy and we quickly got down to business. Economic figures and expectations are regularly shared between member states and the European Commission, so they had a good idea of what our projections for 2011 looked like. Irish authorities had concluded that some increase in the originally proposed adjustments for 2011 would be required, so that the adjustments planned ought to be in the €4.5 billion to €5 billion region. Rehn's staff – he was accompanied by Marco Buti and Istvan Szekely – were convinced on the basis of their different nominal growth projections that a greater adjustment still would be required, and while they were not in the room for the start of the discussion, the ECB were likely to be very keen to ensure a credible frontloaded adjustment, and were probably thinking in terms of €7 billion or more in tax increases and expenditure cuts in the coming year. Indeed, the opening position of the Commission was that achieving a deficit below a target of 10 per cent of GDP in the coming year – which all present agreed would be important to maintaining confidence and in being able to fund the activities of the Government – might actually require more than that. There were also technical points to do with interest on promissory notes given to Anglo-Irish bank which affected the figures, in particular how those might be treated in the calculation of the deficit.

Rehn's main points were that:

1. Frontloading the fiscal adjustments now would lead to less pain later, because the strong political commitment shown would be more convincing to the markets – he quickly came down to a figure of €6 billion as his bottom line.

2. The different macroeconomic assumptions of the two sides were a problem.

3. Politically difficult longer-term measures were necessary to underpin the credibility of the adjustment – he talked about pension cuts and social benefits.

4. The public and the markets needed early indications not just about plans for 2011 but also for a number of years out to allow them to see the structure of the planned adjustments and plan accordingly.

5. There needed to be a strengthening of the legal framework governing the budgetary cycle – more 'rules' about budgetary discipline, in other words.

6. There needed to be a new strategic plan in place for the banking system, complete with timelines.

Lenihan had no issue with some of these suggestions – they were along the lines of the Government's own plans and intentions – but there were problems with others. The differences in macroeconomic assumptions led to a technical difference between us in reaching the target of a 3 per cent deficit by 2014. (The IMF already believed this was an unrealistic target, but the Commission was not ready for that discussion at that stage.) But even allowing for that difference there was some real space between us on what the 2011 adjustment should be. Lenihan in the course of the discussion had already drifted towards his limit of €5 billion and Rehn had come down to €6 billion, but there the room for manoeuvre seemed to stop. The issue around the promissory notes could be further discussed by technical experts, including in Eurostat (the European Union's central statistics office), but the Eurostat view would of course be independent of the Commissioners.

We got into details – we had all rehearsed this on the flight over. An adjustment of €5 billion in 2011 would probably break down as around €3.8 billion in spending cuts and €1.2 billion in tax increases. We preferred to emphasise spending cuts over tax increases, as they were regarded as less damaging to the overall economy. Some of the spending cuts could come from the capital programme, but a large amount would have to come from current spending, and Lenihan explained that this would probably mean big reductions in health, education and welfare. Education, he explained, is harder to cut because we had a rising school age population. The technical matters could continue to be discussed, but the bottom line for Lenihan was that the scale of overall cuts being suggested by the Commission would mean further cuts specifically in pay and social welfare, which would be deflationary for the economy, as well as significant tax increases for the low paid.

To deal with the final point of the discussion – banking – Jürgen Stark and Klaus Masuch of the ECB joined the group. Stark seemed to be in quite a negative mood – or maybe it was the situation which was quite negative, probably a bit of both. He outlined some 'facts'. The ECB had already provided support of €116 billion to the Irish banks and the situation was getting worse – this was not sustainable. A large amount of money was owed to the Eurosystem via the Irish Central Bank in the form of Emergency Liquidity Assistance – in particular by Anglo. 'Emergency', Stark noted, was supposed to mean short-term and there was unease in the ECB about the ongoing nature of this lending, which had to be re-approved every two weeks. There was therefore an urgent need to consider a restructuring plan for the banking system which should be part of an 'overarching programme' also involving fiscal adjustments. He noted that the Greeks were able to continue accessing ECB funds only because they were in an EU/IMF programme, which gave the ECB some confidence in getting its money back. He again talked about the danger that access to funding would not be available, for example if banks were no longer regarded as solvent, and that there had to be some consideration of other possibilities.

At one stage in the discussion, someone wondered about one-off measures to bridge the gap between the €5 billion limit of the Irish side and the €6 billion minimum of the European side. One-off measures are ones that can generate revenue or reduce spending in a single year, without having a knock-on effect into other years. For example, a 2 per cent tax increase will generate income in the year it is introduced and every year afterwards, unless it is reversed, and so it is not a one-off measure. By contrast, a one-year levy, or the sale of a licence for a lump sum, only impact the budget in the year that they happen. So if you need to reduce your deficit by €10 billion in two years, and in the first year you achieve a €5 billion adjustment, but they are all in one-off measures, the deficit reduction in the second year is still €10 billion. One-off measures are seen as a sort of second-class adjustment – they save some money, always a good thing, but they don't help to make progress towards the longer-term goal. For that reason, they tend to be dismissed somewhat in fiscal planning terms.

The full meeting broke up, but Rehn, Stark and Lenihan had a private discussion. Lenihan came out of that meeting. He thought that the Commission and ECB would accept a slightly lesser multi-annual adjustment than they had envisaged, if we could achieve 2011 fiscal measures totalling €6 billion. In fact, he said that Stark had indicated to Rehn that getting a €6 billion adjustment, with a €15 billion four year target, would be better than getting a lesser upfront adjustment with a larger (€17 billion) four year adjustment. Moreover, Lenihan reported that they would accept several hundred million of one-off adjustments in that €6 billion. The question was, did we have a way to find those one-off measures? I said yes, we probably could, and asked the Minister to give us a few minutes to make some calls – we were going to rummage in the kitchen cupboard to see what cans were at the back of the shelf.

I called the Secretary General of a Department. Can we advance the sale of some licences that were otherwise planned for the following year? Someone called the public expenditure experts in Dublin who proposed a couple more measures. Was there any property we could sell? (It had to be physical property, land or buildings, as sales of shares and stocks don't count towards reducing the deficit in European accounting terms.) We thought too that there was probably some room for manoeuvre hidden away in the debt service estimate prepared by the NTMA, and a very helpful conversation with John Corrigan there indicated that they could indeed make a contribution.

So fairly quickly we were able to confirm to the Minister that yes, we could generate a significant number of one-off adjustments for 2011, mostly using measures already envisaged but perhaps for later years. It seemed we had, if not a deal, a route to a solution that could be worked out in the following days which would probably be acceptable to all sides. When the Department's Economic Review and Outlook was published in the first week of November this adjustment package of €6 billion in year one, and €15 billion over four years, formed the basis of the fiscal programme.

11.

In the Mire

B ut by the end of that month, October 2010, we were still in the mire. The sovereign debt position was not going to right itself any time soon. The decision of the NTMA at the end of September to step out of the market temporarily was the right one – there was no point in borrowing large amounts of money at interest rates that were so high they would themselves start to create fiscal imbalances, especially when we had a significant pile of cash in the bank. But that cash would be gone in a few months. Unless there was some way that market access at reasonable interest rates could be restored, we could expect to see that cash pile eroded until in about three or four months the markets would decide that our funding difficulty was now a funding crisis. And however well Ireland might sing the tune of the bond markets, the Irish sovereign debt problems were unlikely to ease unless the broader international sovereign position also eased. But there was no sign of that, as pressures continued on Portugal and even Spain, though to a lesser extent. And just as the developments in Greece had had a devastating effect on willingness to lend to Ireland's government or banking system, the combination of circumstances in Ireland risked creating a contagion effect in other parts of Europe.

This situation had been made worse by events at Deauville around the middle of October. There, among a range of other suggestions for future European policy, the French President and German Chancellor decided to support a package of measures for European economic governance, several of which were controversial. To much of Europe these decisions seemed rude and high-handed. Discussions were going on in other fora, in particular at an ECOFIN meeting, that same weekend, and the joint announcement seemed designed to make those ECOFIN discussions redundant.

For Ireland, and other countries in more immediate danger, these economic governance issues were important, but not the main issue arising from Deauville. Because amidst all of the other matters dealt with at Deauville was a declaration that in the case of sovereign debt crises there would in future be:

> ... *un traitement ordonné des crises dans le futur, comprenant les arrangements nécessaires pour une participation adéquate du secteur privé.*

> ... an orderly treatment of future crises, to include the necessary arrangements for an appropriate participation of the private sector.

This meant that there would in future be a mandatory system of orderly defaults on sovereign debts. There was uproar among policymakers in various parts of Europe who felt that the French and German governments had taken too big a leap, without consulting their partners, and pre-empting a discussion between European finance ministers which was about to take place. This approach would have big implications – it ought to have been discussed, it was argued.

In market terms, the problem was this: if investors believed that instead of being able to rely on the determination of a country to repay them, whatever their difficulties, they could now expect that the same countries might be *required* to default on the same bonds, in certain circumstances, then one would have to place a lower value on those bonds. Moreover, and worryingly, speculators had a very strong incentive to 'short' the bonds of countries in difficulty because if the pressure on the market created by the shorting activity led to a request for a bailout, then they (the speculators) could not lose. The same kind of speculative activity that had burst apart the exchange rate mechanism in the early 1990s might drive a wedge through the Eurozone.

Jean-Claude Trichet was one of those most opposed to the Deauville approach. So far as I know, he has not published a full memoir of his time as President of the ECB, but he has penned a series of articles for the *Nikkei Asian Review* covering the period in summary. In one of those articles he says:

> ... the so-called Deauville doctrine embodied the idea of compulsory private-sector involvement: Any government having recourse to the European financial help would have to obtain debt relief from its private-sector creditors as well. Since any country in potential difficulty was subject to this rule, it frightened traditional investors and excited speculators, who saw the move as guaranteeing profits for short sellers.[42]

Very quickly, press officers rushed to make clear that this was not about the current situation in Greece or Ireland or any of the countries in difficulty at the moment. Rather, this was about how new crises would be dealt with.

But the damage was done. Now, market participants must consider that the policy position of the two most important Eurozone countries, and therefore shortly of the Eurozone itself, was that sovereign defaults might not just be acceptable, but might actually be mandatory, before external public sector assistance would be made available to a country in trouble. These comments from an investment analysis produced by RBS in early November makes the point:

> This private sector participation risk has always been a nightmare scenario for EMU in our view – and has all the hallmarks of making tensions a self-fulfilling prophecy. As we relayed earlier this week ... this changes the very nature of EMU and the risk taking in sovereigns and their banks. In short, this would mean an assessment of EMU sovereigns on much more standalone basis and a basis where the usual adjustment cushions of FX and central bank rates are not available.

It should be said, however, that there are some who do not regard the effect of Deauville as having been so negative,[43] and it is hard to separate the Deauville factor from everything else that was happening around that time, but it is certainly the case that many people with an interest in the issues regarded the Deauville announcement as damaging to confidence.

Nor was there any improvement in the banking situation. Funds continued to flow out of the banks over the month,[44] and the exposure of the Irish banks to the ECB – a good proxy indicator for the liquidity strain on the system – continued to mount.

Against this background it was understandable that the ECB was worried. At every point of contact with Irish authorities the tone and content of ECB comment on Ireland seemed to become more strident and panicky. In this period what I regard as an increasingly hectoring tone began on the part of the ECB. They would make assertions of their policy position that seemed to be largely based on their own belief of how the world should operate and the desire to protect their balance sheet.

In fact, as Masuch told me at some point, the ECB was very concerned that their exposure to Ireland was rapidly approaching 100 per cent of Irish GDP. A default of Irish banks on their debt to the ECB would have meant that losses would be shared among Euro area central banks, and indirectly by citizens of the member states. In his view, this was not only a major risk for the credibility of the ECB and the public support for the euro, but also gave rise to questions of fairness.

Over the following months I heard more often than I care to remember assertions like, 'ELA is supposed to be short-term and cannot continue', or, 'funding to a Government-owned bank could be seen as monetary financing and monetary financing is contrary to the Treaty'. Worse from the Irish perspective, there might be talk of penal interest rates being charged to banks which were relying regularly and over a longer period on emergency ECB funds. We would often be reminded that the funding of Irish banks relied on the acceptance of different types of assets as collateral by the ECB – and the collateral rules or their interpretation in the Irish case might change. So amidst the massive support and genuinely helpful assistance of the ECB in maintaining some stability in the financial system, there was this heightening of tension and increasingly strident rhetoric.

And although all of this seemed unpleasant and less helpful than we might have liked, to a significant extent the ECB was correct – things were definitely getting worse, and they were right to worry that Ireland was not doing enough to address the problems. This was not for want of effort, but rather because the scale of the problems was overwhelming the resources available to deal with them. The ECB worried that they would be expected to finance Irish solutions, but without finance there were no solutions. And without solutions, the ECB's exposure in Ireland would get worse.

Thinking about the ECB

At the time I thought there were two main flaws in the ECB's thinking. The first flaw was a belief among some in the ECB that if only Ireland would do enough frontloading on the fiscal front – more austerity – that the whole position would stabilise. This was based on an assumption that greater deficit reduction would be seen by the market as very positive, and that funding for the sovereign would improve leading to greater scope for the Government to address banking problems. They anticipated a need for further large capital needs in the banks, and felt that if there was a sufficient programme of fiscal consolidation bank recapitalisation might be managed without calling into question the State's debt sustainability.[45]

But the problem was that with a generalised weakening trend in the market, not just for Irish but for all peripheral (and some less peripheral) countries' bonds, it was unlikely that any reasonable fiscal effort by the Irish authorities would reverse the trend. There was a better chance that a credible four year plan would help to alleviate the situation, but if the ECB's panicky state of mind became known this too could to lead to market weakness. The only way to achieve a turnaround in market sentiment would be if the Irish banks' liquidity continued to be supported, and the Irish government's credibility was underpinned by planned actions over a period of months, not days or weeks – a turnaround was going to take time, it was as simple as that.

A second key flaw as I saw it was based in the design of the ECB's central banking functions and their interaction with the other national central banks within the Euro area. One of the functions of a central bank is to act as a lender of last resort (LOLR). This means that in cases where a bank does not have enough cash or deposits to meet its obligations on any given day, it can go to the central bank for funds, and this is a perfectly normal element of banking systems (as explained earlier). In the case of the Eurosystem – the euro area's national central banks and the ECB itself – this system is supplemented by the facility for national central banks being in a position to offer emergency liquidity. So if a bank is in big trouble but still solvent (or being kept solvent by a Government), it can go to the national central bank for funds. In this case, though, any losses arising if the bank eventually went bust would be a loss for the national central bank.

Moreover, during the crisis period, the ECB insisted that every country in Europe would promise to make good, immediately, any loss incurred by a national central bank in giving ELA. This means that when a bank is in trouble, it is a burden on the national fiscal position, unless the State and the national central bank are prepared to see it go bust, with all the damage that might do. Moreover, as the ELA has to be approved or, more precisely 'discussed and not rejected', every two weeks by the ECB Council,[46] and as the ECB's view is that this type of funding must be seen as short term, there is pressure to find a way to put the bank in trouble on to an even keel, or to wind it up in some way.

In a case where a single bank is in trouble, in an otherwise stable system, this approach makes a lot of sense. But when a whole banking system is in difficulty – at the same time as national fiscal problems – it is potentially a recipe for disaster, as shown below.

First, the greater the strain in the system, the more the burden of supporting it is passed from the collective ECB level to the much weaker national level. In other words, at the very moment when national systems are weakest, they are being asked to take on the heaviest loads.

Second, the insistence that Governments back the national central banks means that there is a growing (and potentially truly enormous) contingent liability for the State at precisely the moment when it is least able to accept such a burden. In such circumstances, asking the State to give more support to its banks, or to take over the task of liquidity provision from the central banking system, is quite simply asking it to do the impossible.

Third, the ECB's 'theological' insistence that a bank which has been recapitalised with government paper – precisely because it is in difficulty – might be seen as creating a potential breach of the Treaty prohibition on monetary financing means that any Government trying to cope with the confused and frightening mix of circumstances in a financial crisis cannot rely on a stable policy position and ongoing support from the ECB. In the Irish case, the ECB did allow ELA to continue over a long period – which was very helpful – but at all stages the ongoing support seemed under threat from this perspective that the funding might be deemed inappropriate and discontinued.

At any time, the ECB could block ELA at national level or limit access to ECB funding. Worse, because it sees itself as independent of Governments, the ECB will not 'do a deal' – they will demand action on a particular issue on a particular basis, but any reassuring noises made in private will not necessarily be accompanied by firm confirmation to the market that support will continue. Thus it can be very difficult to plan the appropriate action under these circumstances.

Of course, the ECB would say that all their rules are derived from Treaty provisions, and the legal issues are complex. But to me, the interaction of the Treaty provisions and how they were being interpreted with the complexities of the situation gave rise to serious doubt about their suitability for a crisis of this nature. It certainly made it more difficult at national level to get the maximum benefit from ECB and central bank support.

One could certainly question to what extent some of the elements of the ECB rules are essential features of the Treaty, though the Treaty does make the maintenance of price stability the ECB's principal function. This means that even in the middle of a financial crisis threatening the very existence of the currency, it does not have financial stability as its principal purpose.

The irony is that despite its apparent reluctance, the ECB did in the end provide enormous assistance to Ireland and other countries over a medium-term horizon, and allowed the continuing support of nationalised banks by ELA and ECB funding. And ECB staff who were later among the visiting teams in Dublin consistently put a great deal of personal effort into helping us to deal with a difficult situation. Basically, they wanted to be part of the solution for Ireland. So overall the ECB acted in many ways which were supportive, even while their communications sometimes seemed to be undermining the Government and its efforts. It was a strange mix. But perhaps they would say the same about us?

12.

A Letter from Mr Trichet, a Visit from Mr Rehn, and Messages from Korea

Many of the elements of the description in the previous chapter of the ECB's policy position can be seen in the letter sent by Mr Trichet to Brian Lenihan on 15 October 2010 (see Appendix).

In the first paragraph, Trichet says, or rather seemed to me to be saying, 'okay, we are glad you engaged in discussions with the Commission as I asked and that the ECB was involved in that, and we are glad too that we have agreed between us an appropriate level of fiscal consolidation over time.'

But in the second paragraph he gets more to the point of this letter. He is more formal, but in effect he can be paraphrased as saying, 'but your banks are still shot and we don't like it, and just so you know we are not obliged to keep supporting them, especially if conditions worsen and you in Ireland don't play your part'. And in the third paragraph he could be interpreted to be saying, 'and by the way, we can also block the provision of ELA, so again Ireland needs to be doing its part'. But he does say in the fourth paragraph that Ireland cannot expect this level of ECB funding 'permanently' – so at least he is not pretending the situation can be fixed overnight. Finally, in the last paragraph he is in effect underlining that the fiscal package that has been agreed has to be adhered to, or the consequences could be dire.

Lenihan's reply came early in November. Or rather, it didn't. Lenihan did write back to Trichet, but most of Trichet's letter had not demanded a reply, but rather was setting down a position, so Lenihan's letter did not even try to deal with Trichet's points directly.

Instead, Lenihan's letter, which I believe I had a hand in drafting (but no longer remember the specific details), seeks to enlist Trichet's help. It points out in different words that, 'yes, we in Ireland are in a very tough spot, but we are doing all we can, as evidenced by our recent fiscal announcements. But we are not being helped by interventions such as the Deauville declaration, and indeed other pronouncements by senior politicians in Europe. Maybe you, as President of the ECB, could help calm things down?'

At this stage, the possibility of a bailout being required is of course on the minds of both men – how could it not be? By the date of Lenihan's letter, the yield, or effective interest rate, on Irish 10-year bonds had climbed to nearly 8 per cent, compared to less than 5 per cent three months before, indicating the growing strain on the State's potential to fund itself, and there had been no let up on the banking front, with fund outflows of around €2 billion in just four days.[47] But neither man was calling for a bailout yet through this exchange of correspondence – there was still time to see to what extent the market would be persuaded by the new fiscal plans.

Rehn's visit of 8 November 2008

A few days after Lenihan sent that letter to Trichet, Olli Rehn came to Dublin. Of course, he had a programme of other meetings also while in the city, including with the Taoiseach, but in the Department of Finance we were focussed on the meeting he was to have with us. Rehn and his team, including Istvan Szekely and Stephanie Riso from his private office, were met by Minister Lenihan, myself, Alan Ahearne and Cathy Herbert.

Some of the discussions were fairly technical, but important just the same. There were differences between Irish Government and European Commission economic forecasts, for example, which had to be resolved or explained. Rehn was accepting of the proposed €6 billion fiscal adjustment for 2011, but he wanted to see real and convincing changes to the structure of the economy in the Government's four year plan then under construction.

Rehn also wanted there to be some provision in the plan for additional fiscal adjustment if the economy underperformed relative to our forecasts. Lenihan agreed to this, given that he was not willing to put into the plan a €17 billion adjustment over four years, which would be what was implied by the Commission forecasts. All cuts hurt, he said, so he did not want to cut harder than he had to. But there was discussion of a wide range of structural and fiscal adjustments. Social Welfare, public sector pensions, the tax base, the difficulties of making cuts in the hospital services, even water charges came into the discussion of what might be done over the next four years.

There was a good deal of consensus, but not total agreement. VAT increases were a problem for Lenihan because of the danger of driving trade across the border into Northern Ireland. Rehn was suggesting earlier publication of the proposed four year plan, with very specific measures. Lenihan was concerned that publishing the plan as early as 15 November would leave too big a gap between the plan and the Budget in early December.

In this meeting there was a discussion about a bailout programme as a real possibility. Rehn was in favour of a programme, perhaps to be announced around the same time as the four year plan. Lenihan noted that Ireland was still well funded, and it was not entirely clear that a programme would be required, though he could countenance some sort of precautionary facility, and an associated economic and fiscal programme. Moreover, there was some level of agreement that technical work in relation to the funding and banking situation in Ireland could go ahead. The day after Rehn departed from Ireland that work started, but at that stage even the Commission was talking about a programme of work over 'the next couple of weeks' that could identify and resolve differences of understanding between the potential programme parties.

But there was no decision at that stage, and Rehn was not pushing for an immediate commitment to enter a programme. Instead, the apparent goal was to be well prepared for a potential decision, perhaps on a precautionary basis and around the time of publication of the four year plan, which was not to be for two or three weeks yet.[48] There seemed to be time for an orderly discussion and proper democratic decision-making.

That changed.

Korea

Suddenly, strange things started to happen. Lenihan, in discussion with a very senior Minister from another European member state, heard that Ireland was apparently becoming a feature of important discussions among world leaders.

This was to be expected, but what was surprising was that it was being suggested in Korea, where the G20 meetings were taking place, that Ireland had already decided to seek a bail-out. The Minister to whom Lenihan was speaking had wanted to know what would happen next, now that this decision had been made.

Lenihan was a bit shocked – we had made no such decision. Someone over there, at a forum where Ireland was not represented, apparently took it upon themselves to announce a decision Ireland had not made. Messages came from all around. Parliamentary Questions were put down – is it true that Ireland is currently negotiating a bailout? Dan Mulhall, the Irish ambassador in Berlin, spoke to a high ranking German official, now a senior figure in the Brussels system, who had been given the same story. Mulhall gave the party line, then checked back with base to see if that had changed.

Meanwhile, I got a phone call from Christopher Smart in the US Treasury who had heard we were in bailout discussions with the IMF, also from sources in Korea. I emailed the IMF. Could it be that our precautionary discussions up to now were being misrepresented deliberately? They replied that all internal discussions in the IMF were highly restricted and they were going to tell Smart that there were no programme discussions ongoing.

An Irish contact in the IMF sent a message to Michael McGrath, in the Department of Finance, to let us know the kind of speculation that was swirling around among IMF executive directors. He included material, apparently from a global financial firm, saying that intensive discussions were under way with a view to final decisions in the Eurogroup on 16 November.

All of this was clearly interfering with the proper conduct of business. Because of the messages emanating from Korea, my colleague in the Department of Finance, Jim O'Brien, indicated to the chair of the Euro Working Group – a gathering of very senior officials, which often led policy discussions on serious difficulties within the Euro area – that the Minister did not feel a discussion of Ireland's situation should be on the next Eurogroup Ministers' meeting.

There was so much momentum, and specificity, behind these rumours that it seemed to us that there was a serious attempt being made by high level individuals, either in the European institutions or in the member states, to force Ireland's hand. It did not seem to have emanated from French colleagues, even though the Germans seemed to have got it from the French. The Americans said they got their information 'from Korea'. Rehn's staff were of the same opinion as us as to the outcome of the 8 November meeting, so presumably the rumours were not coming from them, and the IMF officials we were dealing with also seemed puzzled by the situation.

And, of course, all of these rumours had real impact. Not only did we have to worry that market confidence in Ireland would be damaged, but there was real damage being done to the democratic process. At this stage, it seemed highly unlikely that we would avoid a bailout package. And, in fact, it seemed unwise to try to avoid it. Bond yields were heading for 9 per cent,[49] flows were continuing from the banks, and we had insufficient resources to deal with the scale of the problems – getting some help from elsewhere seemed like the logical thing to do. But this was not a decision for officials, or for a single minister. This was something that should be decided by a cabinet, considered properly and debated in the Oireachtas – and someone was trying to rob us of the time and space to do that.

Or so it seemed, at least. It is one of the saddest things about modern Government that in an era when we speak so much about accountability, transparency, freedom of information, and when real progress has been made in these areas, the unattributed leak, or campaign of leaks, protected by the anonymity of journalists' sources, can be used by often unelected and unaccountable people to damage reputations, to muddy waters, and to create a sense of crisis to force the pace of decisions that ought to be made in a considered and deliberate manner.

If it is the case that hidden 'sources' were using these leaks of inaccurate information to bounce Ireland into a bailout (which was sadly by then inevitable anyway), then the people concerned were not just undemocratic, but anti-democratic. They ought to be asked to explain their actions, but they would first have to admit them.

Who was in Korea, announcing falsely that the Irish Government had decided to seek a bailout?

Who, in Korea or elsewhere, was taking these false rumours and putting them into the hands of media and financial commentators?

Were any of these leaks being made directly to Irish journalists, and if so, what can they tell us?

And why did journalists not challenge the source of these leaks? They know full well that behind every leak is a strategy of some sort, so why were these 'stories' reported so uncritically with such little consideration of the possible agendas at play?

13.

Talking about a Programme

The Sunday after Rehn's visit, 14 November 2010, a group of civil servants from the Department of Finance – as well as teams from the NTMA and Central Bank – boarded a Government jet for Brussels. It is most unusual for civil servants to use the Government aircraft without the involvement of a minister in the mission. Apart from humanitarian actions, the only other case I know of was in 1993, and that was connected with a meeting of the European monetary committee to discuss Ireland's depreciation at the time of the 1992/93 currency crisis.

The purpose of the jet was to put Irish officials in a stronger position to engage in serious discussions without having to worry about scheduled flight times and the like, and no doubt more importantly to avoid the speculation that might be generated by the sight of civil servants and central bankers on a flight to Brussels early on a Sunday morning. The flights between Dublin and Brussels, even at the weekend, are heavily used by European and Irish officials, so it was unlikely that someone would not see such a large delegation of officials and put two and two together. During the 92/93 currency crisis, it had been reported to us that some journalists were – quite enterprisingly – ringing around various European member states' finance ministries on a Friday evening asking to speak to individual members of the European Monetary Committee. If they were all out of the office at the same time, that might mean they had all gone to Brussels for an unscheduled weekend meeting to decide on a currency realignment. Similarly, if myself, the Governor of the Central Bank, the head of financial regulation and the CEO of the NTMA were all seen on a flight to Brussels during November 2010, someone would certainly have jumped to the conclusion that this was to be a big weekend for bailout decisions.

In fact, we had an important but more limited mandate than that, and certainly had no directive to arrive at any decisions. We were to discuss the banking situation to see what common conclusions could be arrived at in relation to how we might start to repair it, and we were to engage with the European Commission, the IMF and the ECB about what type of terms might be available if there was a decision to seek the assistance of an EU/IMF programme.

The meetings this time took place in the functional office space of the European Commission in Beaulieu in the southeast of Brussels. They lasted for two days, and much of the discussion in which I was involved went around in interesting circles – neither side wishing to show their hand too early. I was in a room, for most of the time, with Patrick Honohan and John Corrigan on the Irish side (sometimes others joined us). In separate rooms, various teams were ploughing through an agenda of work on more technical matters (especially on the banking system and on fiscal expectations) and reporting back to us occasionally. In the same room as me were Istvan Szekely, Ajai Chopra of the IMF and Klaus Masuch of the ECB – these were the senior faces of the Troika we would find ourselves dealing with most closely in the coming years. We would normally expect also to have seen Ashoka Mody, of the IMF, who had been tic-tac-ing with us in previous weeks, but he was in Washington to finalise terms of reference for any possible IMF mission to Ireland. I had not seen Ashoka in some months. He had been shot and seriously injured the previous year, apparently by an intruder as he returned to his home after a day's work, and was still frail, but was nonetheless preparing to come to Ireland if there was to be a mission.

By the end of the first day of discussions a few things were becoming apparent.

- It was clear, for example, that neither the IMF nor the European emergency financing facilities could provide bank liquidity – that would have to come from the ECB.[50] The ECB would hint, go close to a promise that if we joined a credible EU/IMF programme they would continue to fund the Irish banks,[51] but they would not make this part of any explicit agreement.

- It was clear too that the people in the room had no mandate to discuss the interest rates to be paid – the IMF rules were fixed and the EU and EFSF facility rates would be a matter for the member states to decide together.

- There would be major obstacles to agreement. It seemed likely that demands to change our corporation tax rates would be made by some countries. Others might seek collateral for their loans, which could create enormous practical, political and legal obstacles.

- There were limits to the scale of the programme – about €65 billion was the number in mind, based on a combination of an assessment of how much funding Ireland might need for a three-year programme and the amount that EU officials believed might be raised, after discussion with some of the member states concerned.

While on the one hand, the EU/IMF staff were pressing for greater certainty about Irish intentions, we were anxious to be able to report back to Dublin on the likely shape of any package. In other words, if the Irish Government decided to request a bailout, what type of conditions would apply? This was very important, because once the formal request had been made, Ireland would lose much of its bargaining power.

Towards the end of that afternoon, the IMF produced a note on the elements of a programme – it lacked detail, but could be fleshed out the following day. There was nothing highly objectionable, and most of the measures envisaged by the IMF's 'elements' would equally be built into any sensible plan that we might design ourselves. The Minister was checking in with me from time to time and I was able to relay this message to him.

I had been very clear in the discussions about our views on the corporate tax issue. We were not able to concede anything on that point and it could not be a condition of any programme. How could we put the Irish economy back into a stable situation if we were to undermine the export sector from which the necessary growth would probably come? And why would partners who wish to help us think that this would help? It seemed more like using our temporary weakness to extract long-term competitive advantage.

The Commission was also clear that this was not their demand,[52] and they were simply indicating that this point was likely to be pressed by some countries who might insist on its becoming part of the conditionality of a programme. On that basis I indicated that there might be no agreement on a programme any time soon. I turned to Ajai Chopra and asked him if an important element of the Irish economy's growth model was put at risk, would the IMF be part of that programme? Chopra, helpfully, said simply that he did not know the answer to that. I had put that question to Chopra because I knew that at least one major country had indicated that its representatives at the IMF would resist any attempt to make corporation tax concessions part of the deal, and I hoped that the message might have been passed on.

Later that evening, in a quiet corner of a very busy restaurant off the Grand Place in Brussels, myself and Honohan, Chopra and Masuch had dinner as guests of Szekely and his boss, Marco Buti. We went over the day's events and the prospects for Ireland and Europe. Walking through narrow side streets on the way back to our hotel, Patrick Honohan told me that while I was washing my hands, Buti had taken the opportunity to tell him that I was being unrealistic and that we would have to concede on the corporation tax issue. He was not saying, I believe, that such a concession would be formally part of the conditions for a programme, but rather that it might be a strong background factor in the negotiations. I was irritated by the indirect nature of the message, and I hope in retrospect that I did not take it out on Patrick. But maybe Buti thought the direct approach would not work, and that it was important that we understand the realities.

Discussions continued the next day and we fleshed out more detail – not of the programme, since there was none at that stage, but of the likely demands of the EU/IMF parties in the event of a programme. What kind of structural measures, for example, would they be looking for? Would they have any difficult-to-meet demands that were not already anticipated in the ambitious structural reforms the Irish Government were already planning for? It seemed not. The fiscal pathway they had in mind was in line with that which had already been outlined by the Irish Government, and the structural measures were not out of line with those we were already considering in the drafting of our four year plan. I was able to tell Lenihan as much and he was reassured.

The problem issues were clearly going to be in the banking area. Matthew Elderfield reported that after two days of intensive discussion, questioning and debate, the EU/IMF team, who it seemed to us had expected to be able to find flaws in the capital exercises already carried out on the Irish banks, were in fact somewhat satisfied with the information they were being given. There were no big obvious flaws in the work done to date on which we had based existing capital calculations.

But in some ways that left the situation even more complicated. Even if these potential new partners could be persuaded about the appropriateness of our methodologies, the simple fact was that the market was acting as if the banking system remained fundamentally broken. There would have to be considerable further discussion, including in relation to reducing the size of the sector and fixing the loan to deposit ratios so that Irish banks had a much more balanced mix of assets and liabilities, and indeed more discussion about the level of capital in the banks and how it could be addressed in a way that helped to provide stability. In particular, the ECB took the most sceptical line, and stressed the need for a thorough and credible exercise for assessing capital needs.

Overall, though, these two days of discussions had achieved quite a bit, and I had a strong sense that the people in the room would be reasonably good partners in the future. They each seemed personally committed to helping to resolve Ireland's problems, and to be open to a cooperative and open relationship.

There was one point of disagreement, though, towards the end of day two, I believe. Masuch said that in view of the ongoing rapid deterioration of the situation in the banking sector, his bosses in the ECB would now hope and expect that the Minister for Finance would very quickly announce a decision to enter a bailout. I think everyone in the room at that stage believed a bailout was inevitable, and in some ways this was not a strange request, suggestion or whatever it was. But I had to explain that they had been talking to an official, working for a Minister. There were others to be consulted and reassured – the Government would have to decide on this, not just the Minister. I knew from Lenihan that I could tell Masuch that we were committed to working towards a very quick decision, and I did so, but there were questions unresolved at the end of this two-day discussion which could only be resolved at the level of the Eurozone and ECOFIN. Masuch was reassured, I think, by our promise to work quickly and he accepted my arguments, but I remained a little surprised by the expectation that I would have been able to convey something close to definite decisions that day.

We arrived back at Baldonnel in the early hours of Tuesday, 16 November. My plan was to get a few hours' sleep, be up early and ready to brief a cabinet meeting that morning, before heading back to Brussels that evening with the Minister. Four of us got into one taxi to go northside, to be greeted by a chatty and inquisitive taxi driver. We were, of course, extremely coy about our business abroad, and when the Minister rang to talk about the day's events I reminded him I was in a taxi, so he mostly asked questions to which I could give a simple yes or no answer. Still, as he dropped me off at my house, the driver said to me, 'you go and get a good sleep, I have a feeling we'll all be wanting you rested this week'. So much for secret missions!

Ministerial discussions

I knew from emails over the weekend that the speculation about Ireland's entry to a bailout package was extraordinarily intense. The Department of Finance Press Officer had indicated he received no fewer than 25 calls from journalists before 11.30 on that Sunday morning, 14 November, for example.

But I had been working or travelling non-stop for two days and I was not aware that two Ministers had denied in quite a stark way that there were any negotiations going on. So I was surprised to be asked by a Minister whether our weekend discussions had indeed amounted to a negotiation. I responded, so far as I remember, by noting that I had no mandate to decide anything, but that I was discussing possibilities and asking questions, and the other side was doing the same. None of us could make commitments, but it did have the characteristics of a negotiation.

I understood the context of this question better later. Two Ministers, Dermot Ahern and Noel Dempsey, apparently after a direct briefing from my boss Brian Lenihan, had denied very publicly that any bailout discussions were ongoing, and the two Ministers were subsequently left looking uninformed or, at best, unforthcoming. Clearly, the communication at Ministerial level over the weekend had not been clear enough to prevent them walking into trouble. I wondered if Lenihan had been as upfront with his colleagues as they might have expected, or if there had been a misunderstanding.

I simply don't know the answer to that question, but I do know that the situation was extremely difficult for everyone concerned. Agree with journalists' queries that we were negotiating for a bailout and parties which wanted concessions from us in return would be at an advantage, because once we had announced it there would be little bargaining power left.

Be too coy, and the public would later feel misled. Tell too many people about the discussions in Brussels and risk a leak and further market disruptions. No good options.

The fact is that there were talks going on about the potential for a bailout, but they were preliminary at that stage and aimed at outlining an agenda, and some limits, for further discussions that could then lead to a decision. It was, at that stage, still just talks about talks. But the direction was very clear.

Then matters moved even more quickly. Minister Lenihan and I reported the outcome of the Sunday/Monday discussions to the Cabinet on Tuesday. Unusually (it arose only a few times in my career), I was asked to participate in a short part of the Cabinet meeting. The purpose of the meeting was to give the Minister clearance to negotiate at the Eurogroup and ECOFIN meetings that week. Immediately after the Government meeting, the Minister, myself, Jim O'Brien and a small team headed back to Brussels to be in place for the Eurogroup discussions that evening.

These were tough. There was great pressure on Lenihan to agree immediately to request an EU/IMF programme. From the point of view of other Ministers there seemed little point in a delay. What was Ireland waiting for?

Well, the answer to that question was simple enough: he was not yet in a position to do a deal. At the same time as they were planning to put considerable resources behind the Government's efforts to restore the Irish economy, some of the member states were adopting a threatening stance in relation to key elements of our business model, such as demanding changes in our corporation tax structures, as discussed earlier. In addition, there were parties in the discussion who had been anxious to require Ireland to adopt much tougher fiscal targets, perhaps harsher than the economy and the people could withstand. Others wanted to impose collateral requirements on Ireland, for example the pledging of specific assets against loans, a process which would have been enormously disruptive and counterproductive. There was also a need to see if the ECB could be persuaded to be more helpful still.

There were no indications that the ECB or any of the other parties could be persuaded to make a general long-term bank liquidity facility available, but that left a big gap in the programme. Up to now, the fiscal crisis was driven only in part by the banking crisis: the reversal in the fortunes of the banks had led to big capital requirements that imposed large one-off additions to the National Debt. However, the deficit reduction effort was mostly arising from increased social spending arising from the recession and the huge decrease in revenues – just as the demands on the Exchequer had risen, its resources had plummeted.

However, the banking situation posed huge risks that had to be addressed before lenders would come back into the market for Irish Government paper. Even if the deficit could be stabilised over time, we needed to address the banks' ongoing problems, including their funding. If a programme was to work, Lenihan at least needed to be persuaded that the ECB would continue to fund the banking system. If this was not to be the case, a very different set of decisions would be required.

Moreover, Lenihan did not have the Government's permission at that stage to agree to request a programme. It was clear that such a request would have to be made at some stage, but Lenihan did not have a *carte blanche* that the democratic process could not be entirely set aside – he would have to report back to the Government.

There was one concession he could make, however, especially since the demands for corporation tax changes seemed to have been set aside for the moment at least, and since the demands for collateral appeared to be coming only from a small minority. Up to now, the discussions had mostly been taking place in Brussels. Lenihan could reassure the Euro-group ministers that we were moving in the 'right' direction by allowing the symbolically important step of meetings taking place in Dublin, where they could be better informed and more extensively serviced, which would include all of the Troika parties, including the IMF. And he could promise that the Irish Government would make its decision very quickly. Thus it was that the parties announced that there would be a series of 'short and focussed consultations', aimed at determining the correct next steps for Ireland. Crucially, these were to take place in Dublin.

The agreed statement of the Eurogroup included some important language from an Irish point of view. First, there was a general statement that Ireland was working hard to address the crisis, intended to reassure markets about future direction, but also to acknowledge real efforts made already. Then there was a welcome for the fiscal outline of the forthcoming four year plan:

> The Eurogroup welcomes in particular the announce-ment by the Irish authorities that their four-year bud-getary strategy will be frontloaded by €6 billion in 2011 on a total consolidation effort of €15 billion.[53]

This indicated the Eurogroup's acceptance of the broad outlines of the fiscal consolidation – in other words, no additional austerity beyond that already planned.

However, they would expect that the four year plan would also include significant structural adjustments to the Irish economy. This was in line with what the Minister already had in mind, so was not a threat to Ireland's position. However, although they were accepting the Irish fiscal plan, there remained some doubts about whether it would be sufficient over time, so they wanted there to be annual reviews which, reading between the lines, would also allow for further fiscal measures if required:

> Together with the structural reforms that will be announced in the strategy, this budgetary adjustment should allow Ireland to return to a strong and sustainable growth path while safeguarding the economic and social position of its citizens.

> We nevertheless invite the Irish authorities to include an annual review in their strategy that will allow them to cope with the implications of less favourable macro-economic developments were they to arise.

As far as the banks were concerned, the statement noted that market conditions had not stabilised and more efforts would be needed – any programme would have to deal in detail with the banking sector.

Overall, this was not too bad for Lenihan. He got a day or two of space to consult the Government, consent that the main fiscal and economic plan would be on the lines he was already planning, and other potentially difficult demands, including on tax, were set aside at least for the moment (though some were to come back a few months later).

Short and focussed consultations

That was a Tuesday evening – very quickly staff from the European Commission, IMF and the ECB started to arrive in Dublin for discussions that were to commence on Thursday. This swiftness of movement was possible because, of course, they were on standby, and indeed arrangements had been made some days before, on a precautionary basis, to ensure that all IMF staff who might need them could get visas and would pass through the border entry formalities properly but without fuss.

There was a huge amount of work to be done, and a lot of people to be involved in doing it – the IMF, Commission and ECB each had a substantial team, so there were probably close to 30 Troika-related people in the city at a time. And of course there were dozens of Irish officials involved as well.

This process was, of course, a first for the Irish team involved. The IMF staff benefited from the experience of their organisation as to how to manage these kinds of discussions, but I understood that some of them were new to the management of an IMF programme. Szekely, now working for the Commission, had been a programme manager previously while working for the IMF. Masuch, who I understood was in close contact with Mr. Trichet and the ECB's Executive Board, had recent experience as ECB mission chief, working with Greek authorities on their adjustment programme. But humans settle into routines very quickly, and the pattern of discussion with the Troika over the next week or two followed a pattern set in the first couple of days.

Each day a complicated programme of work would determine which teams would meet which Irish officials, often with several meetings running in parallel, and at the end of the day the senior staff would meet in my room in the Department of Finance, with a few sandwiches and soft drinks from a local shop (for some, the only 'proper' meal of the day, I suspect) and run through the events of the day, discuss any major issues arising and the general direction of the discussions, before breaking up to have further meetings with our own teams and to arrange events for the following day. There were occasional bilateral discussions with individual members or small subgroups of the Troika teams, and all of the senior Irish officials – and the Minister – were on constant standby as needed.

While the discussions were due to get under way, there was some surprise news. Patrick Honohan, the Central Bank Governor, telephoned RTÉ from Frankfurt. He announced to the Irish public, without first notifying the Minister for Finance or the Government, that he expected these discussions to lead to a very substantial EU/IMF bailout package. Exercising his own discretion and the independence of his office, he decided to make a more explicit statement than the Government had been able to make up to then. It seemed to take the public by surprise. Despite all the speculation and the announcement two days previously that the Troika would be coming to town, there was a real surprise for many in Honohan's declaration that the negotiations to take place would lead to a loan of tens of billions of euros to Ireland, which the Government would have to accept.

This put the Government very much on the back foot as far as public relations were concerned, but it also provided some clarity to the situation. As I said to the Oireachtas Banking Inquiry when I was asked, I would have preferred to have an hour or two's notice of Patrick Honohan's intervention, which I would have used to prepare a response that could be issued by the Minister. But I do not think that Honohan's radio interview made a great deal of difference to the ongoing negotiation, though had it been made a couple of days earlier, it certainly would have. It is one of the ironies of modern governance that we often place a high premium on independence of regulatory agencies, then complain when they act independently. One suggestion made in relation to the Honohan interview was that it was done at the behest of the ECB to put

Ireland at a negotiating disadvantage. But knowing his personality this was not likely, and Honohan had the opportunity at the Oireachtas Banking Inquiry hearings to debunk this. I had come to know him pretty well as Governor over – at that stage – more than a year. I was quite happy that his motivations were honest and appropriate.

Another surprise was the arrival on Saturday, 20 November, of a further secret letter from Mr Trichet. This letter was a bit of a puzzle. It was an explicit threat to withdraw funding from Irish banks – even through the mechanism of ELA, from the Irish central bank – unless four conditions were met:

- Ireland had to request assistance from the EU/IMF.

- There had to be decisive fiscal, economic, structural and financial sector measures.

- The package had to provide for capitalising banks that needed capital, and

- The Government had to guarantee to repay any losses of the Irish central bank on ELA.

Why was this a puzzle? Quite simply because the ECB was deeply involved in all the ongoing discussions and was fully aware that these four conditions were about to be met. In retrospect it is easy to attribute a 'bullying' attitude and behaviour to the ECB, and yet there seemed to be little to gain from sending a letter that contained nothing new. Maybe it had been decided to send the letter earlier in the week and by the time all the Departments of the ECB had struggled through the legal and political nuances, it had become less relevant but still had to be sent. I just don't know.

And certainly if the letter had been sent a few days earlier, it would have had real relevance. Since Trichet's previous correspondence, banking outflows had continued and the past week had witnessed some very large movements of funds out of Irish banks. The ECB had a right to be concerned, and was very anxious to see a programme moving ahead as quickly as possible. But as a party to the discussions, it was not, I believe, necessary for it to send this correspondence.

However, it can at least be said that this letter was a clear and open piece of communication, a fairly direct warning/ threat, based on the ECB's own understanding of its rules and role. If pressure is to be exerted, it was much better that it come in this form, rather than in non-transparent leaks to the media by persons unknown, of the type discussed earlier.

Moreover, it could have been that the ECB was concerned that the Irish government might yet withdraw from the idea of a programme at this late stage. In practical terms, this was very unlikely, but it would explain the letter. It also has to be remembered that at this stage the financial future of Portugal was still in play, Spain and Italy might be next to feel the effects of the sudden increase in aversion to risk of the bond market, in which case the challenge to Europe's resources might have become overwhelming. Europe had good reason to want to see quick decisions in Ireland.

In any event, Trichet did not have to wait long. The Government met on Sunday, 21 November, and decided to request EU/IMF assistance. That meant that the talks which had already been taking place to decide whether there would be a programme would now formally become talks about the basis of the assistance.

Terms of engagement

We had to decide how to deal with our visitors. On the one hand, they could be welcomed with open arms as the providers of huge amounts of money to keep the Irish State from going bankrupt. On the other, they could be viewed suspiciously as people here to rob us of our sovereignty. Work with them, or treat the whole process as a cunning game? Share information more or less freely, or guard it with proprietorial zeal?

To me, the answer was clear enough: we were entering into a business relationship. Indeed, this was to be our most important business relationship, and the basis of it was that a group of people representing countries from all over the world were going to come to Ireland to help us out. Yes, there would be problems and some of the demands of the visitors would be unpalatable, perhaps even inappropriate. But we had to consider what would be a success for us, but also what would be a success for them? Actually, for the EU/IMF people on the ground in Dublin, their interests were quite closely aligned with ours. They wanted to be associated with a successful support programme that led to Ireland being back on its feet as quickly as possible. If we dealt with them professionally, explained our situation, demonstrated our competence, they could be expected to engage positively with us. Moreover, they could become our best ambassadors in their various head offices, fighting our corner in Washington, Brussels and Frankfurt.

We had experiences that informed our thinking. There was a clear analogy between the rescue of Irish banks by the Government and the support by the EU/IMF of Ireland's State. And in the case of the banks, we already knew that a suspicious non-trusting relationship had high costs. In any event, it was our intention to try to get the EU/IMF team to buy into Irish plans for dealing with the crisis, and this would require us to win their trust. Moreover, if we developed some goodwill, then when we did have a disagreement with any one of the parties to the Troika, we could enlist the help of the others in persuading the people concerned.

Basically, we needed the money, we needed the programme to work, and this was much more likely to happen with an open cooperative approach – albeit within that framework we would certainly have to assert ourselves and be tough about what was important for us.

Minister Lenihan was entirely in agreement with this approach, and was ever-present in the Department for consultation and direction, and of course to rein us in if he felt we were being either too difficult or too accommodating to the other side in the discussions. As the days of negotiation rolled on, I usually spoke to him daily, sometimes for hours, about developments, our strategy and tactics.

One member of the Oireachtas said around this time that it would have been better to have Silvio Berlusconi negotiating for Ireland than myself, because Berlusconi was a wild card and thus a greater threat to the parties on the other side of the table. Since then, however, the Irish programme, for all its unpleasantness, has come to be seen as a success in allowing the country to turn around. Could a different negotiating stance have been even more successful? We will never know. Although the Greek Government, during the course of 2015, experimented with more of the 'wild card' approach and the economy and banks there took a major hit, their situation is quite different and one should be slow to draw analogies. But just as 'Ireland is not Greece', I am no Berlusconi. I am okay with that.

On 18 November, as we were about to start negotiations, I prepared some comments for my senior management colleagues that reflected my views on this. My notes had five main points in relation to the new relationship, which I now summarise:

- Deal with them openly – we need them to understand our position.

- But commit to nothing – the key decisions to be taken were so important that the Government would have to take them, not civil servants.

- Find flaws in the visitors' thinking, politely and tactfully. After all, we needed their plans to be good plans.

- But also find solutions, and be open to the expertise and experience of these people.

- Work hard and avoid letting personality get in the way of any work problem.

In other words, I was committing the Department of Finance to working with our partners to make an appropriate programme work, rather than to accepting it on paper while seeking to subvert elements of it behind the scenes, which might have been an alternative route. In this, I had the support of the Minister. But before we could commit to a programme, we had to design one, and negotiations on that were ongoing.

The negotiations were very intensive. Teams of staff worked in the Department of Finance in Merrion Street and the Central Bank building in Dame Street to feed the Troika machine with the information it required. The Troika teams worked through their programme of queries at a technical level. It was not an audit, but there was a close interrogation of our policy positions, our figures, our ability to deliver. But it was also a very significant process of negotiation,[54] and for the most part it was between people with a more or less common view of the world. We might have differences of view, for example, on fiscal policy or on economic adjustments, but in truth the differences were small enough. There was a significant pressure on us to abandon our fiscal forecasts instead of the somewhat more pessimistic IMF or European Commission forecasts. For the IMF, this would simply mean that the programme partners were operating from a common forecasting base, but since they were happy, even on their own figures, with the proposed pace of adjustment in the deficit, this would not imply any change in the amount of austerity to be demanded of the Irish people in the coming years. However, European rules were more 'automatic' in their operation. If we adopted new forecasts, and these forecasts did not show us reaching a 3 per cent deficit level by 2014, it might be more difficult for us to resist the pressure to commit to 'do more' austerity in future years. But there was no disagreement between the parties that a significant adjustment would be required each year for some years to come – the only discussion was about the pace of adjustment – and we were able to agree with the Commission and the ECB on the basis of the 'deal' done some weeks before in Brussels.

There were also ongoing discussions on the appropriate structural adjustments needed in the economy. I don't recall any great controversial debate in this area at this point, but we were being just a little coy. These discussions coincided closely with the finalisation of the Government's four year plan, and that work was going on in parallel. We would later come under some pressure to merge the two processes, so that the 'plan' would in effect be the EU/IMF programme – I will deal with this further below.

The issue of the rate of interest to be paid on the EU/IMF loans was also a significant one, though in part these discussions were for the Eurogroup level rather than the technical

173

level. I am afraid that I don't remember the sequence of events on this issue very clearly, but the Irish side was unhappy with the rate of interest being suggested. The IMF's rate was fixed in the IMF rules – there was very little discretion, and apart from some technical adjustments that might be possible at a later stage, absolutely no willingness to adjust these rates on the part of the IMF.

There ought to have been more scope at EU level. There the interest rate was determined by the cost of borrowing of the European Union and the European Financial Stability Facility (EFSF), from which we would borrow, plus a margin that was to be decided on a more 'political' basis. Much smaller loans had been made to certain countries under the EU's Balance of Payment support mechanism at close to the cost of funds (that is, the loans from the EU to the member states concerned were made with little margin over the rate that the EU itself had to pay in order to borrow the money in the first place). But the loans to Greece had been made at a higher rate, and any concession to Ireland would most likely give rise to concessions also to Greece, which was not politically palatable for the lenders at the time. So for the moment it seemed we might have to accept that we were 'price-takers' as far as the interest rates were concerned, but we could aim to go back to the issue later.

The most difficult area of discussion, as usual, was in relation to the banking sector, where the ECB naturally played a major role. This was always going to be the case. In this area the discussions were courteous and professional, but it was more difficult to find consensus. There were a number of key areas for consideration, but the most important for us were liquidity and affordability. To be successful, the programme had to ensure directly or indirectly that the banks would have enough liquidity – available money, in other words – to meet their ongoing obligations. At the same time, the banks had to have enough capital – loss-absorbing capacity, in other words – to allow them to continue to trade and be put back into a position where they could contribute to the economy. Moreover, the continuing dysfunctions of the banking system had to be addressed by an appropriate restructuring of the sector.

But every additional penny that the Government gave to the banks by way of capital was an additional penny that would have to be borrowed, either from the EU/IMF programme or from the market, if we could get access to it, and repaid with interest over time. The danger was that while we could not afford to lose the banking system, we could not afford to save it either. So while it seemed we would have to put more money into the banks, we had to keep the amount as low as possible while still allowing the system to be repaired.

The ECB, in particular, had a different view of the problem. They regarded it as so important to fix the banks that they were inclined to want a much bigger intervention in the banking system (in particular in the form of additional capital injections and faster asset sales) than had so far been shown to be necessary. Masuch argued that fixing the banks with a strong upfront recapitalisation would be crucial to support the economy.

Moreover, the ECB wanted us to take a large chunk of the money available from the EU/IMF programme at a high interest rate, and hand it to Anglo, so that Anglo could pay off monies owed to the Central Banking system, on which they were paying a quite low interest rate. Whatever about putting more money into bank capital, the suggestion that Anglo repay low interest loans with money borrowed by Ireland at a high interest rate seemed to provide benefits to the ECB – being consistent with its interpretation of the Treaty and its mandate, and reducing its unwanted exposure to Ireland – but such an action would be of no benefit to the Irish situation, only adding to our costs.

A similar sort of debate arose in relation to bank deleveraging. It was clear that there was a significant shortage of people willing to fund the Irish banking system, so the cumulative loans issued by the banks far exceeded the deposit base available to fund those loans. In the past this imbalance had been rectified by the banks borrowing money from the wholesale money markets and issuing bonds to bridge the gap. But those wholesale loans and bond investments simply weren't available any more and, in any event, had proved to be very unstable funding sources at a time of crisis. As all of these wholesale funds had been withdrawn, the Central Banking system had filled the gap, but this was not a sustainable way to manage a banking system for the longer term. So banks needed to 'deleverage', simply put, to reduce their loans to customers and other assets so as to put themselves in a more sustainable position. The problem with this was that customers do not repay loans at nearly the speed needed to quickly deleverage the system, so the banks needed to sell subsidiaries to bring in cash and reduce the scale of their operations, as well as to sell some of their customer loans to other parties.

And there was the problem: who wants to buy loans and banking subsidiaries in the middle of a financial crisis? Only people who can buy them very cheaply indeed! And if the banks sell their assets cheaply they make a loss, and that loss reduces their capital, leading them to turn again to the State for even more help. In this way, a fast pace of deleveraging would lead directly to additional demands for State money, in the circumstances of the time. But the ECB was anxious to have a swift pace of deleveraging because that would reduce their exposure to the Irish banking system. They also argued that swift deleveraging and working out of bad loans (together with bank recapitalisation) would pave the way for a strong economic upswing, but it was unclear to the Irish parties how all this extra debt could be affordable. At the same time, the competition experts in the European Commission were also anxious to have a relatively fast deleveraging, because State aid rules required that entities that had received aid would normally be required to downsize and restructure.

This tension, between a natural tendency for the ECB, in particular, but also others to press for a high level of recapitalisation and swifter deleveraging, against a natural tendency for the Irish authorities, the Department of Finance in particular, to be more cautious and protective of Irish funds was to last the whole period of the EU/IMF programme, and indeed elements of the same pressures are still evident today. But back then, there were a number of ways in which we in the Department were able to work with the Central Bank to minimise the risks for Ireland, in ways that were acceptable to the other parties.

The first strategy was to agree that more bank capital would be required. It was clear that the markets were not comfortable with the current capital plans, so more was clearly needed, but we did not need to decide exactly how much more immediately. There would be a transparent and more or less objective process for further analysing the situation of the banks to decide how much capital they would require.

Secondly, to the extent that there was uncertainty about the necessary level of capital, some of the amounts made available to the banks could be on a contingent basis. We could make loans to them that would be turned into ordinary capital if required, but if not required, the loans would be repaid in the ordinary way. These 'contingent capital' instruments were also known as 'CoCos', and early in the discussions Matthew Elderfield – the head of financial regulation – put forward a paper to the Troika parties proposing that CoCos might be part of the mix of solutions to bank capital.

Thirdly, we could put some of the proposals on the back burner. For example, the more difficult suggestions in relation to the pace of deleveraging or the use of programme funding to allow Anglo to reduce its ECB exposures could be quietly but assertively resisted. It helped that, objectively, we could point to the size of the overall programme. It simply was not big enough to meet all the potential demands on it.

14.

Government Formally Applies for Help

Although a lot of discussions had by now already taken place, these had still been, in principle, 'preliminary' ones. Before there could be an EU/IMF Programme for Ireland, the Government would have to decide to formally launch the negotiations – in other words, to formally say 'we want some help here' – and then the programme would have to be discussed and agreed. The first of these events happened after a Government meeting on 21 November 2008.

Most Government decisions are based on a 'Memorandum for Government'. Generally speaking, the Government then discusses the issues with no civil servants in the room other than the Secretary General of the Department of the Taoiseach, or his deputy. There can be exceptions to this practice, and there had been a few during the financial crisis, when officials were asked to provide a briefing to the Cabinet and answer questions, but even then the officials would be ushered out so that the Government could have a private discussion. Such meetings are meant to be entirely confidential to allow the Government to have a free and open debate, and to take a common decision for which they would all be responsible.

The Memorandum for Government for that Sunday set out recent developments[55] giving rise to the need to consider EU/

IMF support, and the likely basis for a deal with them, while noting that various elements were still to be decided.

The likely size of the funding package would be €85 billion, however €17.5 billion of that would come from the Government's own cash, which had been stockpiled in one form or another to allow some flexibility in the markets,[56] so the external package would be €67.5 billion.

Of this, €22.5 billion, one-third, would come from the IMF, and the rest would come from European sources such as the EFSF (European Financial Stability Fund) and EFSM (European Financial Stability Mechanism). By now it seemed the UK would be a willing volunteer to contribute to the European effort also.

The EFSF was a fund put together by Euro area governments the previous summer as a contingency against this kind of situation. Legally, it was a Luxembourg-based company formed by the various Governments with a supervisory Board representing each of the countries concerned. The EFSM was a European Union support mechanism. Since the IMF is a worldwide body, in practice the world in general was supporting us via the IMF, the EU as a whole via the EFSM, and the Euro area member states via the EFSF, each more or less in proportion to the economic importance of the country concerned. So Germany, France, Italy, Spain and the other Euro area countries would be providing support on the triple, by their membership of the IMF, the EU and the EFSF arrangements. The UK, although not in the Euro area, nonetheless volunteered to add more of its support to the mix, but would not do so as part of a Euro area facility – its loan had to be kept separate for domestic political and legal reasons.

That day it became clear that Sweden would also provide bilateral loan support and Denmark followed suit soon after.

These were not members of the Euro area, but would none-theless make their own separate loans available as a welcome gesture of support. Not widely known, however, is that others were willing to help also. Norway made an informal but concrete offer to help, in solidarity with European and Irish difficulties. The European authorities at the time were for some reason not anxious to take this up – perhaps a simple matter of management practicality, but those of us in Ireland who knew about it were very appreciative. There was lots of tough talking and sometimes even threatening behaviour in the negotiations on the programme, but the basic fact was that for most of the partner countries this package was also a genuine show of solidarity.

There was, perhaps, a little less solidarity in the proposed interest rate. Details were still being worked on, but it appeared to be working out at around 7 per cent[57] – perhaps not high relative to the perceived risk of lending to Ireland, but sustaining a large volume of debt at that interest rate over time would be very difficult, and could be counterproductive if it prevented the Irish economy getting back on its feet.

As expected, the plan for a four-year fiscal adjustment of €15 billion – agreed with the European Commission and ECB some weeks before – was likely to be accepted and the calls for a shift in our corporation tax rules were dropped, but not with any commitment that they could not be raised again in the future. At least, they were not to be part of the package.

Banks would be required to have more capital, but to guard against the problems for the State of overcapitalising, described above, the amount of extra capital would be limited initially, and a further stress testing exercise would then take place to determine the final position.

The programme would not provide any bank liquidity (beyond the amount of the capital to be injected), it seemed. We would still have to rely on the ECB for that, but it seemed on the basis of our discussions that at least the ECB – being satisfied with the proposed overall programme – would continue to fund the Irish system and would, we hoped, make appropriate supportive statements that would reassure the markets and bank depositors.

The questions of a requirement to provide collateral and the demand to spend programme funds on paying down Anglo's debt to the central banking system were still in play at this stage, but it was noted in the Memorandum for Government that the Minister would be arguing strongly against any collateral requirement and that there was no money in the arithmetic for the Anglo issue. One could assume that the Minister viewed it as probable that these would not form part of the programme, even if there was still work to be done. It was 'agreed' that Anglo's customer deposits would be moved to other banks, which would reduce their need for official support but increase the need for support for Anglo.

The Government agreed the negotiating positions on that basis and Lenihan went off to a Eurogroup meeting in Brussels where he would update his colleagues and also try to get the less palatable issues off the table. The Eurogroup and ECOFIN ministers and the IMF issued statements welcoming the Irish application for assistance in relatively generous terms, as did Finance Ministers in various member states. The ECB also welcomed it, but was less effusive and certainly did not make any strong additional gestures of support at that point.

The Four Year Plan

The previous days' work had been characterised at the outset as 'short and focussed consultations'. According to the IMF, the next few days were to be characterised by 'swift discussions', but this time with no ambiguity as to the objective of finalising an EU/IMF programme for Ireland.

Much work was already done, as was evident from the detail in the Memorandum for Government on Sunday, 21 November, but there was a good deal more to do. One of the key items on the agenda for discussion was fleshing out the Irish Government's Four Year Plan. The Eurogroup statement on 21 November had indicated that the proposed EU/IMF programme would build on the fiscal adjustment and structural reforms that will be put forward by the Irish authorities in the four year plan, but although the scale of the planned fiscal adjustment had been known since October, the public had not actually seen the plan, which was very close to completion.

The plan was finally published on 24 November 2010. There had been a number of discussions on draft chapters in Government meetings on 16 and 18 November, and the Minister for Finance, as I remember it, had approval to publish the document with whatever minor amendments as might be necessary on the following Wednesday, 24 November.

As it became clear that the document was soon to be finalised, the question was raised at one of the early Department of Finance/Troika meetings whether it would be possible for the Troika partners to see the document before it was agreed by the Government. They argued that since we were in discussions, any document to be published should be agreed by the parties. I resisted this suggestion. First of all, there needed to be some democratic legitimacy around the process – it would not be appropriate for me to discuss a plan in advance of the

Government having finalised it, especially as it was already before the Government. But more importantly, I felt strongly that it would be better for Ireland first to agree its own plan. If the other parties then wanted to discuss the details, fair enough, but let the Irish Government decide what it wanted to do before throwing it open to discussion.

This seemed risky to the Troika parties. A great deal had been made of the four year plan, and if it did not 'fit the bill' for markets and politicians, there could be a dangerous fallout. By this time, though, we knew a lot about the desires of the Troika parties and did not think there would be any surprises for them in the document. So we stuck to our guns.

When the Government finally agreed the text we handed it to the Troika and some Troika staff were told to work through the night to produce a report on the plan by the next morning. As we expected, the Troika were not dissatisfied with the plan – in some ways it was more ambitious than they might have expected of us in regard to structural reform, and it indicated a strong Government commitment to the reform process. Of course, there remained differences arising from the economic forecasts, but the basic thrust was generally acceptable to them.

The plan aimed to raise taxes, reduce expenditure relative to what it would otherwise have been, and to make the economy more competitive and better able to provide employment prospects for its people. But it was a very unpleasant recipe, and was immediately condemned widely.

Bondholders and burden-sharing

During this period there was also a very important discussion in relation to the idea of 'burning' bank bondholders, also known as 'burden-sharing': in other words, ensuring that the bondholders received less than the face value of their loans, thus providing an improvement in the balance sheet position of the Irish banks (if they don't have to repay so much, their liabilities are reduced), and in turn reducing the cost to the Irish taxpayer of saving the banks. So the idea is that some of the losses of the banks would be forced back onto the investors in bank bonds.

It was clear that we would expect investors in the banks' subordinated bonds to take losses. This was already planned. However, the question arose whether to also do so in relation to senior unsecured bonds, which are ordinary debts of a bank. As the bailout discussions got underway formally after 21 November 2010, we thought the IMF would be open to the idea of having some of the senior bank bondholders take losses on their investments. We were pretty sure the ECB would be dead set against and the Commission too was likely to be against the idea, but maybe not so strongly.

There were arguments for and against this burden-sharing approach, but the Irish parties to the discussions – the Central Bank, Financial Regulator, the Department of Finance, and the NTMA – were in favour of the idea at this point in time. But this had not always been the case. Until the autumn of 2010, NTMA advice – accepted by the Minister for Finance – was that to seek to impose losses on senior bank bondholders in Irish banks could be massively counterproductive.

The Central Bank had also previously been cautious on the idea of forced burning of senior bank bondholders. This quote, from a statement by Matthew Elderfield in early October 2010, gives a flavour of official views at the time:

> The Government has made its position clear on this matter and it does not intend to impose losses on senior bond holders. However, this does not rule

185

out the possibility of some negotiations or a liability management exercise agreed by consent. Reflecting on actions by other authorities during the crisis, using resolution powers to impose losses on senior bond holders has, as far as I am aware, taken place only extremely rarely. The current difficult funding position for both the Irish government and the banking system means one should be very cautious about contemplating such a step in the present crisis, never mind whatever legal and constitutional obstacles would need to be resolved.[58]

Media reports at the time noted the official position was not to impose losses, but also that Elderfield's comments left some room for manoeuvre. Great caution would be needed but the door was at least somewhat left open.

The NTMA argument was as follows:

- Any damage to the position of senior bondholders in any of the banks would lead to a situation where bondholders would not invest in Irish banks at all without Government guarantees, and the credit rating of the banks' bonds would be 'irreparably damaged'.[59]

- Moreover, as those who invest in the banks also were the ones to whom we looked to purchase Irish Government bonds – in other words, among the lenders who kept the Government functioning – the prospect of a default on bank debt obligations could seriously damage the Government's ability to borrow.

- As the access of the Government to bond markets was already impaired, it would be a dangerous move to impose losses on the bank bondholders, with all the potential damage that might involve.

By the time of the EU/IMF talks, however, the fiscal, economic and market situation had changed so much that the NTMA's views were changing.

- First of all, by this time, conditions were such that we had temporarily ceased to try to borrow on the bond markets, and assuming successful completion of the negotiations with the EU/IMF we would not need to access those markets for some time. So the risks that might arise if there was a negative market reaction were reduced.

- Secondly, the combined weight of accumulating deficits and bank capitalisation costs were making the debt much less sustainable, and imposed losses on bank bondholders would help to alleviate this problem.

In other words, the balance of advantage had changed.

Against this background, Ireland was now very much open to the idea of forcing losses on senior as well as subordinated bank bondholders. We already had had indications that the IMF would be likely to favour, even press for, the imposition of losses on senior bank bondholders. This was confirmed during a bilateral discussion between the Minister and at least one IMF official. The IMF, or at least those IMF staff we were dealing with, believed that imposing losses even on the senior bondholders was appropriate. In fact, they were very encouraging of the idea, even suggesting that if enough of these losses were taken by the holders of around €30 billion of senior and subordinated bank bonds, the market might decide that the Irish Government would save enough money on bank supports that they could once again regard the government fiscal position as sustainable, and therefore start lending again to the Irish government. If that minor miracle happened quickly enough, any borrowing from the EU/IMF might turn out to be minimal.

It is not as easy as it sounds to 'burn' bondholders: they have property rights protected by the constitution; they are presumed to have made their investments in good faith; and their contracts may not be governed by Irish law in all cases. It is, in fact, quite a tricky thing to arrange while staying on the right side of the law, but in the Department of Finance and NTMA we were looking at these issues and discussing them with our lawyers, who were developing what might be a workable approach. But even the IMF staff felt that there was a dilemma to be addressed: the advantages in terms of direct savings to the Irish purse would have to be set against the disadvantage of creating 'havoc' in the Euro area. Of course, being in the Euro area, this was also a concern for Ireland.

Around this time a world-leading lawyer with extensive experience in this type of operation, Lee Buchheit, arrived in Dublin for discussions with the Attorney General and the Minister for Finance. Buchheit had been involved on the debtors' side in many sovereign debt restructurings since the 1980s and his considerable expertise might well be of use to us in relation to bank debt restructurings. He has published many academic works in these fields, and was later involved in the Greek debt restructurings. In the first half of 2015, he had reportedly again been in discussions in Greece, this time with the Syriza Party's Finance Minister, Yanis Varoufakis.

The Buchheit visit had been suggested and arranged quietly by IMF staff, and the discussions with him were known only to a limited group of people. We needed to explore the practicalities for burden-sharing before having a discussion with the Troika, and we certainly did not want premature leaks to the market. Buchheit met with Attorney General Paul Gallagher and some of his key staff, as well as with at least one of the solicitors from the Arthur Cox firm who were advising us, Pádraig O'Riordan, and also with Brian Lenihan. I attended some of these discussions and was reassured that Buchheit's suggested approach was in principle the same as that being developed by our own advisors.

Even if there were legal obstacles to be grappled with, and even if the IMF staff's presentation seemed optimistic, the prospect of saving significant amounts of taxpayer money by sharing losses with senior bank bondholders was attractive. However, in all our considerations relevant to burden-sharing for bank senior bond holders, there had remained the big question of how to persuade all the Troika parties to agree to this approach.

A plan was in the making. Once the Irish authorities indicated an interest in going forward with burning the senior bondholders, the IMF team in Dublin would put the IMF managing director, Dominique Strauss-Kahn, on alert. He had already indicated to them that he would personally initiate a teleconference with all of the major parties – for example, the appropriate ministers from the bigger countries, the ECB, the Commission – and expected to be able to persuade them of the merits of large scale burden-sharing. There were even indications on 25 November that preliminary discussions between Geithner, the US Treasury Secretary, and Strauss-Kahn had gone well, from our perspective – 'in general so far there has been a positive response', we heard from one source. Strauss-Kahn had apparently met Geithner for a 'one on one' meeting the previous day, 24 November, so perhaps the matter was discussed then.

The telephone call between Strauss-Kahn and various world financial leaders did take place, and like other such international discussions, we in Ireland got no full report on the outcome. It seems clear, however, that in the end Tim Geithner in the US and Jean-Claude Trichet in the ECB,[60] and no doubt others as well, were strongly opposed to any burden-sharing by senior bondholders (despite those initial indications about Geithner). The pro-burden-sharing views of the IMF officials on the ground in Ireland were overruled, and the IMF stance on such burden-sharing became officially negative. The Commission reported to us that the EU position was now that if there was to be burden-sharing for senior bondholders, there would be no programme. The ECB was similarly determined in its views. It was made clear that Ireland was going to have to accept that there would be no senior bond burden-sharing or face an impossible funding situation, and Minister Lenihan told me he would not therefore be recommending to the Government that we attempt it. What seemed possible if we had even some real international support, would not be possible with such blanket opposition.

15.

The Deal

The announcement on 21 November that Ireland would formally enter discussions with the EU/IMF parties to put together a deal did not suddenly solve all our problems. In fact, the parties became more rather than less alarmed about the Irish situation over that week, and the market situation seemed to be deteriorating, most likely due to some political developments. On foot of announcements by the Government's junior coalition partner, the Green Party, that they would be prepared to continue in Government only long enough to complete the programme negotiations, adopt the four year plan and pass the 2011 Budget, the Taoiseach confirmed that an election would be called after the Budget and Finance Bill process was finalised in January 2011.

There were €7 billion of outflows from the Irish banks in that week alone, and Standard and Poor's reduced the credit rating on Irish government debt. Bond yields rose in Ireland, but also in Italy, Spain and Portugal. The prospect of a 'rescue' for Ireland was not assuaging market fears, and these fears were now being exacerbated in relation to other countries too. But discussions were continuing and we started to bring them to a conclusion.

The final 'deal' was captured in various letters and memoranda of understandings comprising a package of agreements,

action plans, time-bound targets and technical understandings, as well as information and reporting requirements allowing the Troika parties great access to Irish data – some of it
even on a weekly basis.

As we came close to concluding the agreed package it was
important to ensure there would be no ambiguity about what
was or was not agreed. The key documents were uploaded
into a computer in the Department of Finance's main conference where they could be projected onto a large screen so that
the senior negotiators on each side could see them. And there,
with the documents on screen, we went through every document paragraph by paragraph – sometimes word by word –
identifying remaining areas of disagreement and, usually, resolving each one on the spot. Occasionally, for a tricky point,
a small group of representatives of each of the parties might
leave the room for a side-discussion to see what resolution
could be found, or a matter might have to be referred, for example, for the Minister's guidance. However, most of the work
could be done there and then, reflecting all the prior preparation that had gone on. As a change was suggested, it would be
entered immediately and the draft revisions would show up
in red print on the screen, and if everyone agreed the new text
we would move on to the next paragraph.

Despite our efforts to reduce the number of people involved,
the fact that there were three parties on the Troika side, and a
number of Irish institutions also engaged, meant that the numbers of people in these sessions rarely dropped below thirty.

In addition to the memoranda that were to be agreed, there
were various contracts to be negotiated and signed with the
EFSM and EFSF, the two European facilities from which money would come, and with the bilateral lenders who had of-

fered to be involved – principally the UK, whose loan was to amount to nearly €4 billion, but also Denmark and Sweden.

Generally speaking, the contract negotiations went without any difficulty, and where there were disagreements they were constructively addressed on all sides. At one point, for example, I received a phone call from my counterpart in the UK, Nick Macpherson, who was concerned that negotiations seemed to have stalled on the UK loan contracts. I told him that indeed that seemed to be the case – there were contract terms being suggested by the UK negotiators that were unusual, or so I thought. Macpherson promised to fix the problems on his side immediately and asked that I tell my team to be equally reasonable – the problems were resolved in a matter of hours, with a bit of genuine good will.

We had been concerned that, relative to the experience with the EU facilities, we were receiving very little documentation from the IMF. The Attorney General in particular was concerned that there might be something to be dealt with that was not yet built into our plans. The two of us and a lawyer from his office, on secondment to the Department of Finance, spoke by telephone to the chief counsel of the IMF around 1.00 a.m. one morning to see what was going on. No, said the IMF man, we don't believe in a lot of extra documentation – if a country does not stick to the rules, they don't get their loans, so we don't need to over-specify everything. That seemed clear enough to us.

The final package was submitted to Government for approval on the evening of 27 November 2010. The Memorandum for Government this time reflected, as would be expected, many of the issues that had been outlined on a provisional basis in the earlier memorandum – the one that had been discussed the previous Sunday and which sought permission to enter this phase of the talks. The Memorandum for Government also contained, as appendices, letters from the Governor of the Central Bank and from the CEO of the NTMA recommending that the Government agree to the proposed EU/IMF programme.

The Memorandum for Government that day outlined the negotiations which had gone on in the previous week and outlined the main elements of the proposed package:

- A total funding package of €85 billion.

- €17.5 billion of that to come from Irish sources, including by drawing down cash from the National Pension Reserve Fund.

- The balance of €67.5 billion to be made available over three years by the various external agencies involved, but principally from the IMF, the EFSF and the EFSM. About €5 billion was expected to be contributed to the mix by way of bilateral loans from the UK, Sweden and Denmark (but, of course, this was in addition to their contribution via the facilities of the EU and IMF).

- There was to be a notional split of the facility, so that €50 billion would be available to fund the state and the remaining €35 billion to fund bank supports – it was stressed that it was not expected to use this amount.

- Now working out at around 6 per cent when converted to fixed rate funding, the interest rate was regarded as high – 'the Minister for Finance will continue working to secure a lower interest rate'.

- It was noted that there were to be a wide range of conditions to be met, and a good deal of oversight: 'The programme contains a significant degree of conditionality and

a level of monitoring that will be both intrusive and oner-
ous'.

- There was to be no requirement in the programme to
change the corporation tax regime.

- The EU would allow one additional year to reach the general 3 per cent deficit threshold. This would not reduce
the level of austerity envisaged already, but depending on
economic developments, it might mean less pressure for
further austerity measures.

- The economic and fiscal approach in the programme
would closely mirror Ireland's own four year plan published only a few days before – 'The National Recovery
Plan is effectively embedded in the Programme', though
some differences were of course to be expected and were
noted.

Discussions about burden-sharing for senior bank bondholders were still going on while the Memorandum for Government was being prepared. It noted the arguments for re-
quiring such burden-sharing, but also noted that any such effort might destabilise markets and have contagion effects in
Ireland and elsewhere.

The memorandum also outlined the proposed plan for
dealing with the banks:

- Additional capital to be required of the banks – it was noted that the Troika had not identified particular flaws in the
stress testing approach adopted earlier in 2010, but that the
capital ratios for banks would now be increased. Immediate recapitalisations of about €10 billion would go ahead,
and in addition there would be further stress testing to be
carried out on a rigorous basis by external consultants, to

determine a final capital target for each bank. Most or all of the banks would come into state ownership.

- Banks would be required to deleverage – assets would have to be sold where possible and appropriate.

- Additional transfers of land and development loans to NAMA would assist in the deleveraging process, but adding to the upfront recapitalisation bill (this was included in the €10 billion figure noted earlier). Various restructurings of the banking system would also take place.

- Ironically, at the same time as the Troika partners were anxious that there be no burden-sharing affecting senior bank bondholders in relation to Irish banks, they were also keen that Ireland would introduce a bank resolution regime for banks in trouble to mirror developing plans for such structures in the EU. These are structures which normally *require* burden-sharing.

- There was also to be a confidential side letter about a proposed transfer of deposits from Anglo and INBS to other banks. This would take some time to arrange, and the letter was to be confidential because it was important not to frighten depositors, who would be fully protected.

One noticeable element of the programme documents presented to the Government is that while the ECB was a party to each discussion – and not just in relation to the banking system – it was not a party to the agreement. The parties were generally referred to as the IMF and the European Commission *in liaison with* the ECB. In discussions the ECB sometimes acted as if a creditor in their own right (and they had indeed the biggest exposures to Ireland, by far, but indirectly through the banks), but they would not, or could not, be party to any of the agreements. The argument was that as monetary policy was independently set by the Governing Council of the ECB, the provisions of central bank loans could not be subject to any agreement or programme document. For that reason, there was no provision in the deal about support for bank liquidity, a huge gap in the framework.

So, while ECB officials might note in discussions that 'the ECB had played its part in Greece and could be expected to do so in Ireland', and while the Central Bank Governor might be hopeful that the ECB would provide some longer-term liquidity to deal with the ongoing problems of Anglo and Irish Nationwide, there would be no formal agreement from the ECB. We had, it seemed, a tacit understanding with them, and that seemed the best that was available, legally and practically. We were assured by the ECB team that in their view the programme provided very good prospects to ensure sufficient bank recapitalisation, and thus solvency of banks, and sovereign debt sustainability, to allow ECB support for banks to continue. In the subsequent months, the ECB did indeed continue to fund the banks, but this informal reassurance at a technical level was as far as the ECB would go in signalling future liquidity support at the time. John Corrigan of NTMA echoed many Irish views when he noted that the statement of the ECB in relation to Ireland's confirmation (the previous week) that it was entering the programme discussions had been disappointingly muted, and that a much stronger statement of support from the ECB would now be very important.

Announcing the news

I'm not sure what time the Government meeting finished on that Saturday night, 27 November 2011, but it must have been quite late in the evening. Even as the Government was meeting, officials of the Department of Finance and other parts of the Irish system, as well as Troika officials, continued to put the finishing touches to programme documentation, while others waited for the green light from the Government meeting to get on with the practical preparations for announcements the next day. A further iteration of all the documents was circulated again shortly before 2.00 a.m.

The following morning's newspapers were filled with stories and opinion pieces about the bailout discussions. Some of these were very well informed indeed, and journalists had clearly been able to get access to a good deal of information about the ongoing discussions. Some of them had information on the likely interest rate, on bank restructuring and on the failure to reach agreement on burden-sharing with senior bank bondholders, although the 'blame' was laid at the feet of the ECB, rather than any other party who might have been involved in the discussion. Journalist Cliff Taylor made a pithy comment in the *Sunday Business Post* that morning to explain much of the dynamic of the negotiations in the previous weeks: that for the Troika parties, 'Ireland was both a crisis that could spread and the precedent for what happens wherever else it spreads to'. Our European and international partners were riding to our rescue, but Ireland was not the only case on their minds.

I met the Taoiseach that morning or early afternoon to go over the issues for the day. There was to be a formal press conference, at which the Taoiseach would announce the deal, in the late afternoon in the press centre in the Department of the Taoiseach. This was to be followed by a press conference by the Troika partners, for convenience to be held in the same room.

But the choreography of that day was to be considerably more complex than that. Echoing Cliff Taylor's understanding of the importance of this event internationally, the decision on the Irish programme would be an international affair.

- In Dublin, there were to be the two press conferences, as well as the publication of a mini-mountain of supporting documentation, and various media interviews.

- In Brussels, there was to be a meeting of the ECOFIN ministers to endorse the deal and to form a conclusion on how to deal with the ongoing fallout from the Deauville declaration of October, in the context of a new support programme.

- In Brussels and Frankfurt there would be press releases to be issued on behalf of the various European institutions concerned.

- In addition to a joint statement with the Europeans, the IMF's President, Strauss-Kahn, would issue his own statement in Washington.

- In other capitals around Europe finance ministries or prime ministers' offices would make their own comments, all of them hopefully guided by the agreed lines emanating from Brussels and Dublin.

Back in my office some time later, studying the documentation for the programme and most likely pondering the steps that had led us to this point, I got a call from one of the Taoiseach's advisers. He said the Taoiseach had asked would I accompany him on the podium for the press conference later. I said of course, I would not want anyone to have to stand on his own to deliver this particular message to the people of Ireland. He thanked me and was about to finish the conversation when a thought occurred to me – were no Ministers going to accompany the Taoiseach? Would it not look strange if there were not? The Taoiseach's adviser said that he would check the situation on that.

Of course, the natural person to accompany the Taoiseach was the Minister for Finance, Brian Lenihan, but he had gone to Brussels to formally conclude the deal at the European level, on the basis agreed by the Government the previous night. When I went over later to the press conference and entered the little side room where Ministers and others would wait before entering, it turned out that there were, in fact, several ministers: Eamon Ryan, Mary Hanafin and Pat Carey. I was to sit on the podium as was my Department of Finance colleague, Ann Nolan. We lined up in the order in which we were to be seated, but at the last moment the Taoiseach asked me to sit beside him to be able to take any technical questions he might refer to me, or indeed to find relevant papers and pass them to him if necessary. This is quite a normal role for a civil servant in a press conference, but the last minute seating switch meant that I was inadvertently seated above a nameplate for Minister Hanafin and she above mine. There is always someone looking for ulterior motives, and I was asked by a journalist after the press conference if this perfectly innocent change of seating arrangement meant that the Minister had been trying at the last minute to distance herself from the Taoiseach or the decision taken, which of course was an unfair conclusion to reach.

I was much deflated that day. We had seen the increasing danger to Ireland's fiscal sovereignty some time before. I had spoken privately to senior colleagues within the Department of Finance months earlier about the possibility that we would not be able to persuade markets about our future credit-worthiness, against a background of increasingly risk-averse investors, and the need to prepare. I had spoken to the Minister during the summer about the necessity to make greater upfront fiscal adjustments for 2011, and to announce them early. I had initiated the work on the four year plan, so as to have a more complete 'story' to give the markets and the Irish people about how we would emerge from the morass. I had engaged with my civil service colleagues on the need to move their adjustment efforts onto a more aggressive footing, given all the risks that surrounded us. In September, or early October, I had outlined the issues to a gathering of senior civil servants and demanded their active participation in the adjustment processes that would be required. But despite all the effort, it was increasingly difficult to swim against the tide and bit by bit it had become clear that we were going to need outside help.

This new effort might also fail. The complex interaction of expected growth in the economy, planned spending cuts and tax increases, likely bank costs, demographics, economic flexibility and dynamism, political instability, all set against a dangerously volatile international background, made it impossible to predict the outcome of our programme. On the face of it, though, it ought to succeed, but it would require public consent, enormous effort and good fortune. The challenges were so great and the timescales so tight that there was, almost literally, not a minute to lose. There was to be no pause for contemplation. The work that was needed to establish the programme and get it running smoothly would have to start immediately, and I was determined to put all my efforts into making the programme work, and I would expect the same of my colleagues.

Meanwhile, in Brussels, the Eurogroup ministers welcomed the Irish programme and agreed on a compromise in relation to the approach to be taken on burden-sharing with bondholders holding the debt of Governments – as opposed to banks – affected by the crisis. European and Irish policies in relation to

burden-sharing were now so mixed up it is no wonder creditors were uncertain about the risks they held. As of the end
of November 2011, it was Eurogroup policy that in the future
there would be burden-sharing where a country was insolvent
so that the private sector creditors of the country concerned
would have to swallow a loss to help the country back on its
feet. However, this was explicitly not to arise until after 2013
– for any current cases, the policy was that there would be no
such burden-sharing. Irish policy was that no such burden-
sharing would take place in relation to our sovereign debt –
in other words, the Government would not default on any of
its obligations. On the other hand, the Irish Government had
wanted to arrange for burden-sharing on senior bonds where
a bank was insolvent or close to it, while Europe, through the
Commission and the ECB, said no, that must not happen. But
they also said that Ireland not just should, but must, provide
for burden-sharing in the future in the same sorts of cases. It
was against this confusion of policies that the Irish government and the Troika had to 'sell' the Irish programme to the
market.

16.

The Programme of Work

The next four months were very busy in the Department of Finance, Central Bank and NTMA – the economic and fiscal programmes envisaged in the National Recovery Plan and the EU/IMF programme, the preparation of the Budget and Finance Bill, the finalisation and introduction of new banking legislation, all had to be accomplished against the background of a political system that was temporarily distracted by both the election of a new leader in Fianna Fáil, by the decisions made by the Green Party in relation to staying in Government until after the Finance Bill and by the calling of an election and the formation of a new Government.

The programme of work agreed with the Troika parties in relation just to the banking system was enormous. It was agreed that we (the Irish authorities) would do all of the following in just four months from the end of November 2010 to the end of March 2011:

Capital

- Implement the bank recapitalisation measures which had already been announced on 30 September 2010 [details]

- Extend the NAMA programme to include approximately €16 billion of land and development loans in AIB and Bank of Ireland, which had previously been excluded as they were below a value threshold of €20 million. This would help to further deleverage the banks concerned by reducing their risk asset base. The NAMA legislation would be amended to provide the necessary means to do this efficiently.

- Increase minimum capital requirements for named Irish banks (AIB, BOI, EBS and ILP) to 10.5 per cent core tier 1.

- Ensure that AIB, BOI and EBS are – notwithstanding the 10.5 per cent requirement – initially recapitalised to a level of 12 per cent core tier 1 capital, which will take account of haircuts on the additional loans to be transferred to NAMA and will fund early deleveraging by making available €10 billion in the system; the recapitalisation will take the form of equity shares (or equivalent instruments for EBS).

- Design a new 2011 Prudential Capital Assessment (PCAR) stress-testing exercise and complete it on a basis agreed between the Central Bank, the European Commission, IMF and ECB staff. Extensive external consultancy would be used and the methodology used would be published in detail to enhance market confidence and transparency.

Deleveraging

- The Central Bank was also to complete a Prudential Liquidity Assessment Plan (PLAR) for 2011 – just as the PCAR would assess the capital position of the banks with a view to developing a plan for addressing deficiencies, it was intended that the PLAR would outline measures to be implemented with a view to steadily deleveraging the banking system and reducing the banks' reliance on short-term funding by the end of the programme period.

Ambitious target loan-to-deposit ratios, to be achieved by end 2013, would be established for each bank by the Irish authorities in consultation with the ECB and the IMF by end December 2010.

- The PLAR would not only establish target funding ratios for 2013 for each of the banks, but also identify non-core assets and set an adjustment path to these targets based on specified non-public annual benchmarks. Banks would be instructed to comply with specific actions related to their funding targets and adjustment paths.

Reorganisation of banking sector

- A revised strategy for the future structure, functioning and viability of Irish credit institutions, providing for a comprehensive reorganisation and downsizing of the banking sector would be developed in detail and agreed with the European Commission, the ECB and the IMF.

- A specific plan for the resolution of Anglo Irish Bank and Irish Nationwide Building Society would be established which would seek to minimise capital losses arising from the working out of these non-viable credit institutions, but in the meanwhile the Government would be committed to ensuring they met the requisite capital adequacy ratios.

- Legislation on improved procedures for early intervention in distressed banks and a special bank resolution regime (SRR) would be introduced, to be consistent with similar initiatives ongoing at EU level.

Burden-sharing by holders of subordinated debt

- Consistent with EU State aid rules, burden-sharing would be achieved with holders of subordinated debt in relevant credit institutions over the period of the programme. Legislation allowing for this to take place on a forced basis would be submitted to the Oireachtas by end-2010, but it was also possible that similar arrangements would instead be managed on a quasi-voluntary basis, similar to the exercises that were already going on at the time in relation to holders of subordinated debt in Anglo Irish Bank. These exercises would be commenced by end of the first quarter in 2011.[61] A side-letter between the Minister and the programme partners committed Ireland to engaging immediately with bank asset disposals, and to introducing legislation very quickly which would allow the transfer of deposits from Anglo and Irish Nationwide into other institutions, leaving these two institutions as a 'rump' of loans to be worked out. It was agreed that any capital requirement generated arising from the working out of these loans would be met.

There is a great deal that could be written about the process of implementing the programme in the months immediately after the bailout was agreed. It was quite simply a major feat of administration of a type that critics of the Irish public service would probably not believe could be done. Relatively small teams of staff in various public bodies – and also in the Troika institutions and in the banks – shifted huge mountains of work, ticking off one by one the various targets and benchmark actions that were agreed to be done. And this was all done with a high level of co-ordination, a great consistency of effort and with a mutually respectful relationship between the programme staff in the Troika institutions and the Irish parties concerned.

The work to be done by the Troika staff should also not be underestimated. Some of them had simultaneous responsibilities in relation to the EU/IMF programmes in Ireland and Greece, but also in relation to economic surveillance, competition rules or Balance of Payments facility programmes. And this was a new line of business for both the Commission and the ECB, so they had to build on their existing resources to create new teams of people for all of this work – but that took time and was probably far from complete when the Irish programme commenced. In other words, they too were short-handed from the outset.

It was not just the visiting teams of economists and financial specialists that were concerned: in the Commission and in the EFSF new borrowing programmes had to be built to gather in the funds which would then be passed, in turn, to Ireland – and a significant programme of market information and reassurance was required to ensure that these new bodies could find the funds that we needed. It has to be remembered that the EFSF was itself only a few months old[62] and untested, and even though they had been designed to attract an AAA credit rating, there was no guarantee that markets would rush to provide funds each time these institutions issued a new bond. I recall sending notes of congratulations, and thanks, to Klaus Regling in the EFSF and Gerassimos Thomas, who was responsible in the European Commission for the EFSM, on their early bond issues for the Irish programme, and feeling reassured that they had gone without a hitch. (In later months, even with their highly creditworthy status and their AAA rating, the EFSF and EFSM had to continue to work hard to ensure they remained acceptable in the marketplace as investors became even more risk averse.)

Coordination units were set up in each of the principal Irish public bodies concerned to ensure a smooth flow of information to and from the Troika, but also between the Irish parties, and to track progress on the benchmark actions to be taken. Senior Irish officials met regularly and there was a weekly conference call between them and the senior Troika staff, while working and technical calls were happening all the time. As far as banking matters were concerned, it was mostly the Department of Finance, Central Bank and NTMA who were engaged, but the overall EU/IMF programme also involved all the other Departments of Government, and their responsiveness was good. Meetings happened when they were needed, and targets and actions were addressed almost always in good time. The system of Government responded well. In fact, when the IMF published a retrospective evaluation of the Programme in 2015, their evaluation showed an amazingly smooth implementation of all the agreed actions. Just about every single aspect of the Programme was met at the time it was supposed to be met. An important exception will be discussed below.

Tensions

Over the course of those months, and indeed afterwards, there were certain major issues dominating all discussions to do with the banking system. And one of the most important of those was the capitalisation of the banks. As the big date drew closer there were still a number of issues to be resolved, and real dangers in getting the resolutions wrong. The first of these issues was to estimate, precisely, how much extra capital each of the banks would require. The second big issue was how these capital requirements would be met. And both issues had direct implications for the size and sustainability of our national debt.

Assuming the capital requirements of the banks were to be met, mostly, by the Government, and that the potential for capital raising from other sources was limited, at the margin each euro of capital required by any of the banks concerned would translate into an additional euro of cost to the Government. And since the Government had considerably less revenue than it had outgoings, and no private sector lenders, that additional euro had to be borrowed from the EU/IMF partners, and therefore added directly to that national debt. This had two implications. The first was that taxpayers would be asked to repay that euro at some stage, with interest to be paid in the meanwhile. The second was that the sustainability of the debt – the extent to which the Government could expect to manage to live with the mountain of debt that was accumulating – worsened with each additional euro added to the top of the mountain. If the debt got too high, no one would believe the Government could manage to pay the interest on it, let alone pay back all the money. At that point, lenders would refuse to lend to Ireland, or would lend only at interest rates that were too high to afford.

We had already seen, the previous autumn, private sector lenders demanding interest rates that were so high that we could no longer afford to borrow from them. Even the EU/IMF would not lend indefinitely if the debt seemed unsustainable in the long run. And since the interest on the mountain of debt had to be paid by the Irish taxpayer, each additional euro of capital was going to cost them five or six cents per year in interest.[63] So if the additional capital requirement to be met by the State was, say, €30 billion, then the taxpayer would have to fork out more than €1.5 billion extra per year in interest, which would translate very quickly into additional tax hikes or cuts in benefits and services for our citizens.

We were already on the edge of a cliff in terms of debt sustainability, therefore, and the big question was whether this additional capital demand would push us over the edge. But for the person on the edge of a cliff, being able to move just a few inches away from the edge makes a big difference in terms of safety. So saving even a few billion euros from the cost of additional bank capital would make a big difference to our national fiscal position.

Some experts would, with some justification, dispute elements of this argument. They might say that, in fact, if you put too much capital into your banks and it turns out later that this was not necessary, well, at that stage you can take the capital back out. So in this view there really is no great danger in overcapitalising, and having put so much capital in that no one could possibly doubt the security of our banks, they will then be able to go back to their normal business of lending into the economy, which would in turn rebound. In fact, precisely this argument was made, in particular by the ECB, but by other parties too, at various points in our discussions with the Troika. But while there is some truth in this perspective, it seemed overly simplistic to us. In Ireland's circumstance at the time, on the very limits of our borrowing capacity and without certainty that additional capital could be clawed back in the same amounts as it was put in, we did not have the luxury of going too far.

Moreover, even in a nationalised bank, providing too much capital provides all the wrong incentives to the bankers concerned. It says to them, look, here is free money to use to sort out your problems. If you save some of this money, the Government will take it back, but if you spend it to buy your way out of problem loans, for example, well you will have a nice healthy bank at the end of it, and you can expect an easy return to the private sector, where you can tell everyone what a good job you did in cleaning up the old bank. Of course, this is not how all the bankers concerned would think, but that is the direction in which the incentives lie. And people who talked to us about the history of other banking crises did indeed report that some bankers treated State money with less proprietorial zeal than private money.

The big question to be determined, therefore, was what exactly the right, necessary, amount of capital might be, without going too far. In theory, one might expect this to have been scientifically determined by the various consulting groups who had been contracted at huge cost for the purpose, in conjunction with the Central Bank – and their input was indeed key to determining the capital levels. But the science in these areas is not precise and the intuitive preferences of the various parties did of course intervene. It seemed to us that there was a constant pressure from the Troika parties – especially but not only the ECB – towards increasing the amount of capital to be injected, while rushing the pace of sale of assets to deleverage the banking system.

From the point of view of the Department of Finance, our constant interest was not to go too far too fast in disposing of potentially valuable assets. At the bottom of a recession, in the eye of a financial storm, this was hardly the best time to be judging long-term property values or expecting to get a reasonable market price for asset sales. Our constant refrain was 'no fire sales': assets were not to be pushed into an already poor market at a rate which in itself would drive the prices of such assets further down.

The Central Bank was in a strange position here. From a purely institutional point of view, it had the potential to take a position that was contrary to the general interests of Irish taxpayers. After all, additional capital and swifter resolution of banking problems, even at additional cost to the State, ought to have made their job easier. If they were taking only their insti-

211

tutional interest into account, they might well have ploughed the same furrow as the ECB. In fact, the Central Bank senior staff tried very hard to do the right thing, which was to help find the optimum level of capital injection rather than an extreme level. And they tried hard to be imaginative in finding solutions to the problems that came up.

There was thus a constant pull in the relationship between the Irish parties and the Troika, the strength of which varied from time to time, around the pace and scale of capitalisation and deleveraging in the financial system. 'Tension' is probably the best word for it, so long as that word is not taken to imply a negative emotional dispute. Based on the different interests of the people involved in the discussion, and of their bosses back at their respective bases, there were real differences of emphasis.

An example of this constant tension came in a discussion between Jürgen Stark of the ECB, the Minister of Finance and myself. Klaus Masuch, I believe, accompanied Stark who came to Dublin to see the Minister (I think that this was not long after the programme was agreed, but am open to correction) and his main point was along the lines of, 'look, the programme notionally allocates something like €35 billion towards bank rescues, and we think you should be ready to spend that amount'. From our point of view, that was horrific – it would bring the total banking costs up towards €80 billion. But looked at from the ECB point of view, the extra capital involved would have reduced the size of central bank exposures to the Irish banks, since the cash handed over would immediately reduce the banks' requirement for central bank funds – the exposure to Irish Banks was by far their largest country exposure at the time – and would have made the remainder of the central bank exposure less risky, since the extra capital would provide a greater buffer against losses. For them, two birds with one (very expensive) stone.

Of course, the Irish response was clear. We had agreed in the programme to inject the required capital, but that was to be determined by a process of examination of the bank loan books by outside consultants, following on agreed stress tests – we certainly should not be expected to pay more than was determined to be necessary. In fairness, Stark (who tended to stick to his deals, once done) accepted this. But it was clear that just as the ECB would be watching us eagle-eyed for any backsliding on our part on our capital commitment, we would have to watch them for any attempt to ratchet up the capital levels emerging from the technical process, or to force the pace of asset sales beyond what was likely to produce reasonable value.

The bottom line for the ECB in this compromise was that they could expect a real and determined effort by Ireland to reduce its banking system's exposure to the ECB over time, but they could not expect us to cripple ourselves even more than was necessary to do so. So they had to – and generally speaking did – accept that there would be no immediate exit for the ECB from its Irish exposures. But even though they would commit to this approach in discussions, there was never a formal commitment from the ECB, and therefore we always had to be on our guard for attempted changes in their position. Perhaps from their point of view, they felt they always had to be on their guard against any attempt to load the cost of Irish banks on to the ECB in a permanent way.

This natural tension was stretched a little further by one of the last big decisions of Brian Lenihan as Minister for Finance. Even though it had been agreed that initial capital injections into the banks, reflecting in part decisions made the previous

September, would proceed in early 2011, the Minister decided
– towards the very beginning of February 2011 – that it would
be inappropriate to go ahead with these capital injections with
the certainty of a new Government coming into office shortly
afterwards. He told me he did not think he had the democratic
mandate to continue to inject capital when the next Government might take a different view. From recollection, he spoke
directly to Olli Rehn. I know he planned to speak to Trichet
at the ECB as well, but I now understand that the news was
passed to Trichet by Governor Honohan, who suggested to the
ECB President that a tough reaction would be counterproductive.

There was, still, some push-back to this approach, and an
Ireland/Troika conference call was hastily arranged to discuss
the Minister's position. The Troika parties were naturally concerned by the change of plan. The programme was off to a
good start, in terms of implementation, and this would appear
to be an early 'blot' on the copybook. Moreover, there did not
seem to be much controversy about the plan to input more
capital – was it really necessary to delay?

In addition to the danger that a significant delay in implementation of an important element might undermine the credibility of the overall programme, there might also have been
a concern that the delay would defer an opportunity to start
to address the huge Irish banking exposure to the ECB. The
planned injection of capital would have had the side-effect of
reducing the ECB exposure of the Irish banking system by an
equivalent amount, helping to put that very large exposure on
a downward trajectory. In the end, there was a compromise
which everyone could live with. The capital injection would
have to await the new Government, but most of the monies
that would have been applied – about €7 billion – would still

be drawn down and deposited with the banks to ensure that early downward push on the ECB exposures could happen.

Worries about the Programme

A set of meetings in Frankfurt on 17 and 18 February provided an opportunity to review the whole programme with the ECB and other partners, and in particular the banking elements. Myself, John Corrigan and Patrick Honohan engaged over a series of meetings with Vitor Constancio, Jürgen Stark and Klaus Masuch from the ECB, Ajai Chopra from the IMF and Istvan Szekely, Sean Berrigan and Alberto Bacchiega from the European Commission and probably others as well. There was quite a bit of concern that the programme did not seem to be working at this point. Deleveraging was not happening as quickly as the Troika parties would like, the recapitalisation had been deferred and political parties likely to be in the new Government were renewing discussion about burning senior bank bondholders. The ECB accepted that there was a need to avoid fire sales, which was almost a tacit acceptance that their exposure to Ireland could not be unwound at breakneck speed. But they wanted to see real progress. What was being said was that the programme was not delivering, but perhaps there was a sense also that Ireland was not delivering.

On the Irish side there was some frustration, too. Although the ECB was making liquidity available in huge amounts to support the banking system, much of it had to be renewed in two weekly increments, and there was always an element of threat that this would not be allowed at some point. Indeed, rather than moving towards any agreement on providing medium-term funds, the threat to the two-weekly renewal of short-term funds for Anglo was itself renewed at these meetings, as the ECB colleagues pointed to new risks. For example, a legal review of the ECB's conformity with the Treaty was due to take place shortly – perhaps this would find that lending to Anglo was monetary financing, contrary to the Treaty, which would have to be stopped. I repeated, as I often did, that there was nothing at all in the Treaty to support this interpretation. We could not make progress if under constant threat that the ECB would precipitate a disaster.

But the ECB's problem was real enough – they had found themselves by default as long-term financiers of Anglo. They had perhaps hoped that the EU/IMF programme would provide enough funds to repay their lending to Anglo, but the other Troika partners had not wanted this, as it would mean a much bigger programme, and Ireland did not want it because cheap money for Anglo from the ECB was much better than more expensive money from the EFSF.

On top of all this was the danger that Eurostat – the European Statistical agency – might at any stage decide that debts of the banking system would be classified as debts of the Government. Suddenly on all the main international tables, the Irish Government's debt position would look much worse than it actually was, in net terms, and our credit rating might suffer even further.[64] On the question of burning senior bank bondholders, the ECB had obtained their own advice on the legal position in Irish law. They were reassured that, constitutionally, it was not allowable for the Irish Government to arrange for burden-sharing with the senior creditors. I could have explained that we had our own understanding of the constitutional difficulties, and that there might be ways to address them, but I did not want to weaken the hand of a future Irish Government, so I settled on a simpler response: I was fairly sure that the necessary referendum could be passed very quickly if it were needed.

It was not just the ECB who were nervous – the IMF and Commission were also a bit jumpy. And the truth was that so were we. It was a period of considerable uncertainty, and beneath it all was concern about what decisions a future Irish Government would take. Those decisions would have to wait a while, and in the meanwhile everyone was bound to be on edge.

We were probably all too impatient – the programme was not yet three months old and the big actions planned for the end of March could not, of course, have had any effect so far. It was too soon to assess progress in any real way. However, Irish 10 year bond yields were still hovering around 9 per cent, and Portuguese yields were holding at a relatively high 7.3 per cent and showing no signs of easing. Bank outflows had continued. There was no reason to be cheerful. But there was a lot of work in train which had yet to bear fruit.

17.

A New Government

In fact, as far as the programme was concerned the transition to the new Government went smoothly enough. The Dáil had been dissolved at the beginning of February, in line with the previous announcements that the outgoing Government would fold its tents as soon as the Finance Bill was passed. The election took place on 25 February 2011, and the Dáil met to elect a Taoiseach on 9 March 2011, but it was clear a few days earlier that the Government would be a coalition between Labour and Fine Gael. Both these parties had had discussions with the Troika back in November 2008, when the programme was being designed, and it seemed clear that the Troika would have room for negotiation on a number of key areas. In relation to fiscal policy, in particular, so long as the main headline numbers were not to change, the Troika would be quite flexible about how to achieve them.

The programme for Government agreed between the parties noted that the EU/IMF programme had so far not managed to restore confidence in the Irish economy, reflecting uncertainty over the affordability of the rescue package (debt sustainability again) and the unknown potential cost of resolving the banking crisis. It pledged to renegotiate the overall package in a number of areas, including the interest rate payable, and, while many of the measures proposed were in line with existing plans, there was a pledge to halt further transfers to NAMA, and to look at making legislative provision for burden-sharing with senior bank bondholders. The Programme for Government also indicated that no new decisions on capital would be made until the ongoing PCAR assessments were completed.[65]

Even before the new Government was put in place, the political parties who were to form it renewed their contacts with the Troika. Two of their key economic advisers, one each from Fine Gael and Labour, held a significant teleconference with the mission chiefs of the Troika, which I facilitated. The two advisers were not quite yet in a position to formally represent the Irish Government, but they were ensuring that the transition from one Government to the next would be managed in a smooth and professional way. The two advisers were able to point out that the new Government had a large majority and therefore a mandate to take difficult decisions. They noted concerns about debt sustainability, which would have to be discussed with the Irish agencies concerned. They had always been clear that the sustainability of the debt was finely balanced, and they might need to address this. There was also a need to find a 'sustainable direction' on banking policy.

The Commission was anxious to know more about their views on these issues, noting that coming to conclusions was difficult in advance of the completion of the then ongoing PCAR exercise, but there was a general reassurance that the new Government would likely stick to the broad outlines of the previously agreed fiscal policy. Any changes they planned to make with revenue or expenditure implications would be offset by other measures. Naturally, the ECB stressed its perspective on the capital needs of the banks and that it was more optimistic that public debt was indeed sustainable.

The Troika parties at this stage seemed open to some experimentation. The IMF noted that they had been encouraging the EU to consider giving more tools to the EFSF to reduce the negative interaction between the problems of the banks and their Governments, though they acknowledged that even if the Commission was sympathetic, the political climate might not be conducive. Overall, the Troika parties seemed reassured – the new Government would be wanting change, but not in every aspect of the programme, and all sides were talking about the importance of early and more formal engagement at ministerial level and the urgent work on the next steps to be taken. A formal review of the programme was due in April (having been deferred to allow for the election period), but some big decisions were due to be taken even before then.

The new Government created a cabinet sub-committee, called the Economic Management Council (EMC), to manage the flow of information, to facilitate discussion on the economic and financial issues and to prepare for the decisions of the Government. There was a great deal of effort in that forum for a new campaign of negotiation in relation to Europe and the EU/IMF programme, and even though it was going to be an uphill struggle, there seemed to be signs, at least, of a sympathetic hearing from European quarters, if not any actual movement at first.

The EMC was to compose of the Minister for Finance, now Michael Noonan, and the Minister for Public Expenditure and Reform, Brendan Howlin, taking over the portfolio that had been Brian Lenihan's as Minister for Finance, plus some functions from the Department of the Taoiseach. The new Taoiseach, Enda Kenny, and Tánaiste, Eamon Gilmore, were to lead discussions. Various senior officials and advisors were also to be present, and there would be a secretariat in the Department of the Taoiseach. For the moment I was to be present as Secretary General for both the Department of Finance and the nascent Department of Public Expenditure and Reform, until the latter was put on a statutory footing and had its own Secretary General. Despite one or two rocky moments, this new forum very quickly became an effective way to clear business and to ensure both parties in the coalition were at one on policy decisions. It was especially important in the first couple of months of the new Government, when decisions had to be taken very quickly and unity was essential.

The first high level meetings between the new Minister for Finance and key European leaders seemed to go reasonably well. There were meetings in Brussels around Monday, 14 March, for example. Minister Noonan spoke to Trichet on the fringes of a Eurogroup meeting. It seemed to Minister Noonan that Trichet was open to more definitive public statements of support for the Irish banking system following the bank recapitalisation, making clear to markets that the ECB was not going to pull out of its Irish commitments, provided they in turn would see a steady reduction in the ECB exposure to Ireland. Trichet also told Noonan that he understood that fire sale type deleveraging for Ireland was not appropriate and so the ECB was not going to press for very fast deleveraging.

There were more extensive meetings on 14 March with Commissioner Rehn and with Eurogroup Chairman, and Luxembourg Prime Minister, Jean-Claude Juncker (now President of the European Commission). Again, much of what was said from the European side was very positive, and Noonan got an open hearing for the new Government's policies. Even before the change of Government there had been some progress in convincing Europe of the need for lower interest rates on our borrowings. Rehn indicated he was supportive in this regard.

He also agreed that bank deleveraging should be at an appropriate pace – no fire sales, in other words. And he was supportive on the Eurostat problems, though he had some limitations in relation to Eurostat. It was a peculiarity of the system's architecture that Eurostat was within Rehn's administrative domain, but not within his policy control. In other words, their decisions were made independently of the Commissioner. It was nonetheless hoped that that if the ECB continued to classify Anglo as a bank, even if in run-off mode and no longer open for new business, Eurostat might in turn decide to use the ECB's classification for its purposes, so that Anglo would stay off the national balance sheet and its debts would not add to the national debt for accounting purposes.[66]

Noonan also argued that more of the burden of supporting the banking system should be transferred to the EU in some form, but both Rehn and his Director General, Marco Buti, felt there was little chance of progress on that at that moment.

But there was a new fly in the ointment – or rather an old one had re-appeared. The previous Friday, new Taoiseach Enda Kenny had been presented with a joint demand from his French and German counterparts for changes in Irish corporation tax policy, which he had to reject, just as the previous Government had done in negotiating the EU/IMF programme in the first place. But since the French and Germans had made this initiative,[67] all negotiations were going to be complicated by this demand, and potential interest rate adjustments might have to wait for a calmer moment. Ireland could discuss tax issues, could consider the interests and demands of its European partners, but could not allow the programme to be used to undermine its economy in ways which would work against the objectives of the programme in the first place. This tax problem featured again in the discussions with Juncker who, as Chairman of the Eurogroup, was trying to find an approach that might allow progress to continue. That the Irish 12.5 per cent corporation tax rate remains in place even now, despite these pressures on the Irish authorities, perhaps illustrates that there were no easy compromises available to Ireland at that most difficult of times.

18.

31 March 2011 – A Definitive Moment for Irish Banking

The banking announcements made by Minister Noonan on 31 March 2011, less than a month after coming into Government, represented weeks of work by him and the new administration, and very long months of preparation by the Irish administrative system. These announcements mark a key turning point in the rescue of the Irish banking system, the moment at which, with the help of external resources, Ireland finally came to grips with the problem. It was far from being the first radical attempt to deal with the problems of the system, but it was probably the first package of measures that was not later overtaken by events, that did not have to be unpicked or redone in wholesale fashion in the face of the overwhelming tide of events. Now the tide was on the turn, at least as far as the banking system was concerned. But it was not possible to be sure of that at the time. Then, everything seemed still to be very much in flux.

The package of measures announced that day included a number of key policy decisions and some very important specific points. At the policy level, it was decided to:

- Reduce the size of the banking system.

- Produce two new 'pillar banks', based on the existing Bank of Ireland and AIB platforms and create a restructured Irish Life and Permanent. EBS would be subsumed into AIB.

- Ensure that these are highly capitalized, based on the Central Bank's new norms, and ready for the then upcoming new 'Basel III' rules.

- Ensure that the banks are more focused on core operations, and better funded relative to their size, so that each of the 'new' operations would create a split between core and non-core functions.

- Non-core elements of the banks would be sold off over time, but at a pace that would avoid fire sales. This would provide a much better balance between the deposits of the banks concerned and their lending, reducing the reliance on central bank, interbank and wholesale funding.

- Ensure substantial additional capitalization of the banks to meet the terms of the new PCAR exercise being completed by the Central Bank.

- Anglo Irish Bank and Irish Nationwide would continue to be 'worked out' over time in an orderly manner to minimize any further capital injections in those institutions – a further assessment would be carried out the following May (which, as it happens, did not give rise to further capital requirements).

For Bank of Ireland, the implication was that there would have to be asset reductions of about €30 billion over time. As there were some signs of potential for private sector interest in providing capital, they would be given time to explore this possibility. This would help to maintain the commercial focus

225

of the bank and reduce the burden on the State of recapitalization.

The combined operations of AIB and EBS would have to reduce assets by about €23 billion over time. As with Bank of Ireland, AIB would be domestically focused, though retaining its important UK operations.

Irish Life and Permanent (ILP) would immediately commence to sell its life insurance subsidiary Irish Life Assurance, as well as other non-banking assets – there would again be a core/non-core split and €10 billion of non-core assets would be available for sale. The State would provide the necessary capital for ILP, subject to its making its own contribution through the funds raised from the sale of its non-bank business.

For Anglo and Irish Nationwide, there was to be no capital injection – they were not a part of the PCAR exercise. The Government's policy was to continue to allow them to be 'worked out' – gradually run down in other words – over time, and a further capital assessment would be carried out in May 2011. As it happens, that further assessment did not give rise to a further capital demand, but had it done so, there would have been a significant point of tension with the Troika. The end March statement was careful not to promise to put additional capital into these failed institutions. Instead, it said that the position would be considered, if required:

> The Government will then consult with the external partners on the timeframe and means of recapitalising those institutions at minimum cost to the taxpayer, having regard to the financial stability impacts in Ireland and abroad.

More about the background to this approach below.

Following on the work that had been going on in regard to the PCAR exercise, the Minister was able to note that the bank stress tests which had taken place were 'certainly among the most thorough and demanding such tests ever performed in Ireland or indeed anywhere'. This was certainly the case – the work had been thorough and quite comprehensive and not just the results, but enormous amounts of detailed data which allowed market participants to interrogate the subcomponents of the work done, were being published. It was clear that the capital assessment was meant to be very conservative.

But the result was a very significant additional demand for capital for the banks. Noonan noted that the State injection in the banks to date had been around €46 billion, while bank investors had also lost about €70 billion, on some measures, but now a further €24 billion was to be required. It should be noted that this cannot be equated to finding additional losses in the banks which had not yet been taken into account.

The State's investment in the banks would, it was planned, lead to very high level of capital in the banks that we supported. Their PCAR requirements were not only looking at bank loan data from a conservative point of view, but also were aiming at higher targets. Much of the additional capital therefore would be required not simply to cover losses, but also to have higher target capital ratios in the future. In theory, therefore, there would now be additional value in the banks which the State could recoup at some later stage.

But in explaining where the package came from, it may be useful to describe some of the events of that and previous days. How was the €24 billion figure arrived at, and how was it that burden-sharing with senior bondholders was not mentioned?

As regards the question of capital, the basics are simple enough. Starting from an end-2010 base, the Central Bank took account of existing capital and provisions for losses already made, then added in the expected (pre-losses) profit of the banks in that period. That added up more or less to the amount of capital the banks could expect to have without intervention. Then the Central Bank set against that the likely losses over the period, on the basis of the work done by the Blackrock consultants, and the required level of capital to be held at the end of the period, to give a capital shortfall amount, which added up to €24 billion. In fact, this calculation was done twice: once on the basis of an expected 'base case' capital requirement, and base case expectations for profit and losses etc., then it was done a second time making much more conservative 'stress case' assumptions, and calculated against a lower target capital level. This ensured that the banks would have enough capital to weather an even worse storm than was already blowing.

But despite the science, there was a certain amount of subjective judgement and debate about what assumptions were to be made, which also affected the final figures.

It was in these areas of judgement and debate that there was some disagreement between Troika parties and the Irish authorities. It should be made clear that all the parties were fully committed to fully credible and evidence-based capital provision. This was a common starting point. But wherever there was room for debate, the Troika seemed to want to opt for more bank capital – and therefore more cost – while the Irish authorities, being concerned about the affordability of our debt, were anxious not to put into banks a lot more than was necessary to meet the market credibility test. These issues were the subject of intense discussions at a senior level between the Troika mission chiefs, their experts and the Irish authorities on Friday, 25 March and – in great detail – on Sunday, 27 March.

Before the discussion that was to take place on 25 March, I had a call from Istvan Szekely on these issues. He was anxious for my view on how the Government would react to the likely outcome of the capital calculations, which he felt were likely to 'start with a two' – in other words, more than €20 billion. He was concerned that it seemed whenever an issue arose which might push the eventual number higher, the Irish technical staff managed to find offsetting reasons for reducing the number again. I asked him whether, in fact, the proposed increases in capital calculations were being driven by a desire for a higher outcome, or by the underlying 'scientific' approach. He thought it was the latter, but my view at the time – informed by my own contacts – was that we were in fact entering a period of horse trading. The science could only get us so far, and then there would have to be a high level discussion to tie things down. That was what the calls on Friday, 25 March and Sunday, 27 March would in truth be about – to work through the technical issues, but also to finalise the horse trading.[68]

As this conversation was, technically, about what advice the Central Bank should give the Government, much of the discussion was led by Patrick Honohan, Matthew Elderfield and Jonathan MacMahon of the Central Bank, but in the end the figure of €24 billion represented an increase on what the Irish Central Bank would have been comfortable with, left to their own devices, and there was reassuring news that, for the moment, the Central Bank was not expecting any extra capital demand for Anglo or Irish Nationwide. The discussion went back and forth for several hours, with a number of stops for side-discussions and consultations. It became clear that in addition to the technical arguments each party had a view of the 'bottom line'. In particular, a decision to add an extra buffer for potential bank losses in 2014 was outside the original scope of the exercise which was to cover 2011 to 2013. But the €24 billion figure did at least have the advantage of being acceptable to all the parties, albeit begrudgingly in some cases, and large enough to allow the Irish authorities to present the banking mess as being properly addressed. And it allowed the ECB to issue a rather supportive statement soon after the government had announced its plan.

Back to burden-sharing

In a letter to Minister Noonan on 29 March 2011, conscious of the fact that he would be announcing the proposed recapitalisation numbers just two days later, Patrick Honohan laid out the Central Bank's summary views:

- A radical reorganisation around two pillar banks is highly desirable now.

- The newly configured banks will need the extra capital that has been calculated if they are to regain market confidence.

- A comprehensive statement on Government policy in regard to burden-sharing with bondholders of the continuing banks should be made soon.

- But even taking all that effort into account, cost and availability of funding for Irish banks was also dependent on getting the Government finances fully under control.

A second key issue related to the question of burden-sharing for senior bank bondholders. Irish representatives hoped that the ongoing reluctance of the ECB to continue funding the banking system as required could be replaced by a positive and public statement of intent from the ECB in that regard. At the same time, the Government hoped to announce its intention to force burden-sharing on senior bank bondholders in Anglo. So Ireland was asking for more explicit public support from the ECB, as well as a limited reversal of the ECB opposition to burden-sharing, in the Anglo case only.

This ought to have been the easiest case of senior bank bondholder burden-sharing for the ECB to agree to. The market prices of Anglo bonds already seemed to imply an expectation of burden-sharing, so there ought to have been no great shock to the market if bondholders in this defunct entity were to take a loss.

Moreover, there seemed to be some relenting on the ECB's position – the indications we were getting were of decreasing opposition in the ECB to such a move. Although a message received from Jürgen Stark on Wednesday, 30 March, suggested that the ECB was still dead set against burden-sharing for the seniors, even he seemed to allow for the possibility of a purely voluntary burden-sharing. At the same time there were some indications that President Trichet's view might have shifted a little, and for the first time we felt that there might be others within the ECB willing to press the Irish case for burden-sharing.

I will now recount my understanding of some conversations of which I have no note and which I was not a party to, so I am relying on hearsay and am, of course, open to correction. But as I recall what I was told at the time, the Taoiseach spoke to Trichet on the morning of the banking announcement and the latter seemed to have moved somewhat in his position, especially if any burden-sharing in relation to Anglo could be presented as 'voluntary' – market prices seemed to suggest that even a voluntary approach could generate real savings. Trichet would be prepared to put the proposition to his Governing Council, which was due to meet that afternoon in Frankfurt.

Then we got news that Axel Weber, the head of the Bundes-bank, Germany's central bank, and as such one of the members of the ECB Council, had stated in Berlin that morning that it was 'better that Ireland isolates bank deposits, lowers burden on its taxpayers and make creditors participate in losses'. In other words, bondholders should take losses, just as Ireland would wish. It seemed likely that even if Weber was not in Frankfurt for the Governing Council meeting, his view would be influential.

Finally, however, we got the message (I heard it by telephone from an ECB official, but Ministers may have heard it directly, I understand, and the same message was also sent by email) that in fact the ECB Governing Council had decided to make it clear that in the event that we pursued even the merest modicum of burden-sharing in relation to senior bonds – even purely voluntary – we could not expect any supporting statement from them, thus undermining all the power of the banking announcements to take place that day. I felt that was wrong. There had been some logic when the ECB and others blocked burden-sharing a few months earlier, perhaps, but the market situation had moved on, and we were talking about a voluntary exercise and only in defunct institutions.

To the ECB, the benefit of doing the exercise probably did not seem to be sufficient to justify the risks, though these seemed to us to be small. In fact, that is precisely the argument the ECB has since advanced. At the time of publication of the correspondence of October/November 2010 between Trichet and Lenihan, the ECB also helpfully provided its views on various questions that Irish people and others might have about its decisions. They said:

> It should be emphasised that the potential amount of savings that could be made when, in late 2011 (sic)

the issue of burden-sharing of senior debt issued by Anglo Irish Bank went on the programme's agenda, was limited – somewhere between €3 and €4 billion. This should be compared with the risks that the bail-in option would have entailed at that point in time, when market sentiment was severely shaken and there were no clear EU rules on a pecking order in crisis resolution … a bail-in could have had very adverse consequences for financial stability in Ireland, with negative spillover effects on banks in Ireland and other euro area countries.[69]

So the ECB had some real concerns, but the Irish people were going to have to bear the cost of this. Moreover, the ECB position was leaving the new Government without even a modicum of protection from public opinion, which was expecting, even demanding, some level of burden-sharing on these bonds. How were people to sign up to all the negative features of a programme if they did not trust the European institutions to help protect them or the Government that acceded to them? I thought then, and still do, that it was a short-sighted and unnecessary imposition of costs on Ireland. But we will never know who was right, and of course it might have made life more difficult, for example in Italy and Spain, if Ireland had taken the planned steps. Certainly, even on the day of the announcement there were analysts in London predicting dire consequences in the European periphery if any burden-sharing took place in Ireland, suggesting that the ECB were not the only believers in the contagion risks.

Much more positively, later that evening the ECB issued a statement making clear that it would continue to accept Irish Government paper as collateral for ECB operations – making life easier for the banking system in Ireland – and also welcomed the Minister's banking announcements in a press statement made jointly with the Commission and the IMF. But more importantly, they issued a further statement welcoming the package of banking measures on their own behalf, saying straightforwardly that the ECB will continue to fund the Irish banking system. A simple statement, months in negotiation.

So that was another €24 billion for the Irish taxpayer to stump up? Well, not quite. The banks had to get €24 billion of capital, but it did not all have to come from the taxpayer. At the time of the Minister's announcement there had already been a €10 billion contribution from the holders of subordinated bank bonds to offset some of the Irish banks' losses, and the plan now was to force more such losses onto the holders of other subordinated bonds. Moreover, there seemed to be some prospect of getting some private capital for Bank of Ireland from investors who thought the bottom had been reached and wanted to buy bank shares at low prices – taking more risk, but for greater potential reward. Additionally, some of the capital required – some €3 billion of it – would not be injected as equity up front, but would be provided as so-called 'contingent capital', the CoCos discussed earlier. In that form the funds were available for a period of years, if required, but the CoCos held by the Government could be sold by the State to other investors if there was a market for them or, assuming they had not been converted into capital, would eventually be automatically redeemed. The money would then come back to the State.

So the actual injection of capital by the State arising from the PCAR was likely to be well under €20 billion, even before taking into account any private capital in Bank of Ireland and the Irish Life asset sales.

In the nine months between the end of March 2011 and the end of January 2012 some things got worse before they got better, but the March 2011 banking statement marked the turning point in terms of the banking crisis.

In the months after that announcement Bank of Ireland managed to raise significant amounts of equity capital from the private sector, principally through direct investments led by Wilbur Ross and Fairfax, which allowed Bank of Ireland to remain a majority privately-owned institution. These investors provided funds at a time when others would not, and when they first started to sell their Bank of Ireland shares it was at about twice the price they had paid.

At the same time a number of successful LMEs, liability management exercises – yet another euphemism for the process of burden-sharing or burning of bondholders – provided an opportunity for subordinated bondholders to contribute to the capital requirements of the banks. These exercises eventually contributed €5.2 billion to bank core capital, in addition to the €9.9 billion contribution in the period prior to March 2011.

Not all the bondholders went quietly. A group called Aurelius Capital Management tried hard to wriggle out of the same treatment as was applied to other holders of AIB subordinated debt. When the Irish Government declined to engage with them, they commissioned powerful lobbyists in Washington to try to get the US Treasury Department, State Department and members of Congress to pressure Ireland to come to the table. It was amazing how responsive the US system was to the lobbyists – almost immediately we started to receive messages from the US demanding that we should engage with these bondholders. I was so concerned by this that I sent an unusually strong email to a senior official in the Treasury Department, with whom I had a lot of previous dealings, followed by a detailed phone call.

I pointed out that Aurelius were holding up a very important capital raising, and failure to complete that would have broad financial stability implications beyond Ireland. I also pointed out that the Irish public already held the US at least partly responsible for not being able to let senior bond holders take losses, at considerable cost, and would hardly be pleased to hear that the US was also now interfering with the imposition of losses on the subordinated bondholders. I got a helpful response from the Treasury official, and whether because of him or otherwise we had little subsequent pressure from the US Government despite the lobbying. Aurelius were claiming they were going to be badly hit by 'discrimination' by the Irish Government,[70] but they never, to my recollection, showed any real damage and our suspicion was that they bought their bonds very cheaply with the intention of trying to force a legal settlement. In the end, Aurelius had to settle for the same terms as the other bondholders, and payment of their costs, as I recall.[71]

It was a great credit to my colleagues in the Department of Finance and the Attorney General's office that they stuck to their guns in fighting this outfit, sometimes despite advice suggesting that they be bought off. The favourable outcome may well have saved Ireland hundreds of millions of euros, because a failure in relation to AIB might also have interfered with the Bank of Ireland process.

Afterword

A huge part of my job in the crisis period was to provide leadership and support to the various teams of central bankers, supervisors, bankers, advisers and Government officials who were involved in dealing with the banking crisis. The biggest challenge in that regard was to hold them all together and work in more or less the same direction, and I hope that with the help of my colleagues in the NTMA and Central Bank we managed to achieve that much.

This was not as easy as it might seem, however. All public bodies are set up to serve the public interest, but they each are given different legal functions, different powers, different incentives, different reporting and accountability arrangements, that sometimes push them apart rather than together. As one Taoiseach said to me in relation to a growing mini-crisis, 'let's not have one of those situations in which everyone seems to do the right thing, according to their functions, and yet we still get the wrong outcome'. So keeping the institutions working towards more or less the same public interest goals was a constant, almost daily, struggle that occupied much of the time of the senior administrators in those bodies. Any serious falling out between us might have made for an even worse long-term outcome than we had. During my time as Secretary General of the Department of Finance, I really appreciated that people like Patrick Honohan, Matthew Elderfield, John Corrigan, Brendan McDonagh (and I say 'people like' because there were so many others) were so willing to work with me, despite real external strains and occasional points of disagreement. We shared ideas, resources and innovative solutions as far as we could to help the public interest and tried hard to avoid inter-agency games.

And when the combination of domestic and international crises eventually overwhelmed us and the Government had to call for international help – from the IMF, from the European institutions and European member states – I was very grateful that they came, with expertise and money, to our assistance. The narrative that this help was provided only out of self-interest is not true, I think. The European ideal, the drive towards solidarity among European member states, did influence decision making in Europe, and amongst all the valid and invalid criticisms we can make, there is one very important lesson for the future – that the continued existence of these mechanisms, and the continued capacity of European institutions to react both quickly and effectively when needed, provides a critically important insurance policy for every European member state, which none could provide on their own. We should hope that the message that these institutions and states have taken from this period is not that solidarity is costly and difficult, but rather that it helps to deal with crises and is to everyone's long-term benefit.

The people who came as technical experts on behalf of these various international institutions did come with agendas and preconceptions about the Irish crisis, and they did fight their own corner as their bosses in Brussels or Frankfurt or Washington would expect. But the programme overall was to our great benefit and the people who they sent were, I believe, determined to make it work for Ireland. There is no contradiction between wishing that some elements of the programme, some aspects of the Troika's policies, might have been different and appreciating the efforts of those who helped us, individually and institutionally.

I do not have a great insight into the internal workings of these Troika institutions, but I do know enough to suspect that there were internal critics within each – people who were against the programme of support for Ireland and believed that the resources being expended in Ireland might well be lost. The efforts of the IMF, European Commission and ECB mission chiefs and their team members in convincing their own bosses to stick with the programme were, I suspect, important in keeping the money flowing.

They were also important in facilitating the various renegotiations between 2011 and 2013 which gradually improved the deal that Ireland received. Interest rate reductions, loan-term extensions, the final deal on winding up Anglo and the manner in which promissory notes given to Anglo as capital were to be dealt with on its wind up – these are beyond the scope of this book, but together they had an equivalent economic effect to wiping billions off our national debt.

In the Department of Finance, I worked with many officials who were equally dedicated to the management of our crisis. I have already mentioned some in the course of this book. Not everyone, of course, was the same and some had more energy and commitment to offer than others, but as a group I was very proud of them and of my association with them. I recall one moment during the November 2010 bailout negotiations. The annual Budget was to be announced to the Dáil in about two-and-a-half weeks, which seemed like a long way off given the pace of developments that month. But the Troika parties were pressing to accelerate the process and bring forward the Budget, which I did not want to do. The workload of negotiating and organising the bailout, plus producing the Government's four year plan, all involved many of the same people who would work on the Budget preparations, and it seemed to me to be unrealistic to expect them to take on another job. Nonetheless, I went into our Monday morning management meeting and said, 'guys, if we really had to do it – just how quickly could we produce the Budget?' The two assistant secretaries whose teams would have to co-ordinate this feat exchanged a glance and one of them said, 'not before Thursday', and around him his colleagues nodded. I had no idea where they thought they would summon up the energy and resources to collapse the work of 15 or 16 packed days into three, but I was sure they would, proud they could, and glad that in the end they didn't have to. The Budget date was not changed.

And there were moments when they managed to inject a little humour into a difficult situation. In 2011, when the three year EU/IMF support programme was barely started, pessimistic commentators started to talk about Ireland as if it was a dead economy – this programme of support is all very well, they said, but how will they fund their deficit after the programme? The implication was that some thought it was a foregone conclusion that Ireland would not be able to borrow in its own right in three years' time. As it happens, we were borrowing, hesitantly at first then very confidently some months later, by mid-2012, so the doom-mongers were very wrong. But at the time the question was not moot. I drafted what I intended to be a rousing email to colleagues telling them that we were going to beat the bushes for sources of cash, beyond the EU/IMF programme, with a target of finding one more year of funding to reassure markets and to be more than ready when the time came to exit the bailout. I went in to a colleague's room, on the same corridor as mine, and explained the proposition to him. 'We need to set up a working group', I said. 'Yes,' he replied, 'the Johnny Logan Working Group', after the Johnny Logan Eurovision Song Contest winner *What's Another Year*. I did not know at the time that the next line of the song was, 'to someone who's lost everything that he owns'.

When Ajai Chopra, the leader of the IMF team for the programme missions to Ireland, gave his personal evidence to the Banking Inquiry, he gave an assessment on the Irish teams he dealt with:

> On the Irish side, the counterparts at both the technocratic and political level were uniformly superb. They were knowledgeable, dedicated, smart, funny and committed to tackling Ireland's difficult situation.[72]

And the same day Michael Noonan gave his summing up on the Department of Finance at the time he became Minister: 'I found they were grand.'[73]

I believe it's important against this background to reflect on the validity of the now standard narrative that hopelessly inept civil servants, poorly led, were incapable of dealing with our nation's problem and that was the source of the difficulties for our country. That is too simplistic – civil servants and their colleagues in other agencies did things in a month during the crisis which, in normal times, might be the biggest effort of a year. A huge legislative programme, budgets and emergency budgets, negotiations on many different fronts at the same time, hundreds of EU-IMF programme targets, all of them met on time, except where a ministerial decision said 'delay'. This could not have been the case if we were all inept.

And yet we had an enormous crisis, which none of us wants to live through again, and all the reports produced so far identified real institutional failings that had to be addressed. Perhaps the Report of the Banking Inquiry, in preparation as I write this, will do the same.

To strengthen the institution of the Department of Finance, not long after I became Secretary General, I arranged for what became known as the 'Wright Report'.[74] I wanted a reasoned report on the past and a blueprint for a new Department of Finance prepared by people with real independence. The Report confirmed many of the positive views that might be reflected in the Chopra and Noonan comments reported above, but it also made a very wide-ranging set of quite challenging recommendations. There were 50 of them, on topics ranging from the structure and functions of the Department and the mix of skills and educational qualifications of the staff members, to the manner and tone in which the Department should communicate with Ministers, Government and the outside world. They also made some recommendations about the broader environment within which fiscal policy should operate, including in relation to the setting up of a fiscal advisory council.

The overall message was that even if there were, in fact, some good foundations, we needed to build a quite substantially different structure on those. Before I had left the Department of Finance I had made some good progress on some of these recommendations, such as opening the Department to outside economic expertise, drafting in various specialists from both public and private sector, encouraging the establishment by Government of the Fiscal Advisory Council,[75] taking steps to professionalise the HR function and so forth.

Some of the other Wright Report recommendations remained to be addressed and some were overtaken by events.

In particular, since the Wright Report was not published by the Minister of the day until March 2011,[76] after the election, its recommendations in relation to the structure of the Department were overtaken by new decisions by the incoming Government.

So could it all happen again?

There has already been a lot of institutional reform, both at the national and at the EU level. One of the first institutional reform initiatives aimed specifically at the regulation and supervision of banking was in relation to the Central Bank where the Central Bank Act 2010 was to provide Honohan and Elderfield with a modified, more unified structure, in the Central Bank system, fully integrated under one Governor and one board. This was accompanied by much larger staff complements for supervisory functions, development of a new separate enforcement function and senior level recruits to reinforce the existing team, and allow for the development of a new management and supervisory culture. The Central Bank has more resources, is better equipped, differently trained and its efforts are differently applied than before the recent crisis, though it has to continually work to maintain staffing levels against quite a high turnover of supervisory staff.

But at the European level, the banking supervision and crisis management regime has changed enormously. The principal supervisor of the main Irish banks, in relation to their solvency and soundness, is in fact no longer the Irish Central Bank. Instead, the supervisory power resides within the ECB and is carried out through what is known as the Single Supervisory Mechanism. The quality of supervision of Irish banks will in future depend on the quality of that new structure.

There is also a new Single Resolution Mechanism (SRM) to deal with failed banks. As part of that system, a Single Resolution Board (SRB) (already in existence by 2015 and to be fully operational from 2016) will take most of the decisions about how to deal with any large failing bank and implementation will rely on so-called National Resolution Authorities. It will have access to a resolution fund, eventually to exceed €50 billion (perhaps not big enough to cope with a large Europe-wide crisis in itself, but probably large enough for many eventualities). But in fact the fund is not intended to be the first resort for a bank in difficulties. Instead, as one European Council press release says:

> The aim is to ensure the orderly resolution of failing banks without recourse to taxpayers' money. This will involve both a systematic recourse to the bail-in of shareholders and creditors ... and the possible recourse to a single fund fully financed by banks.[77]

Even though there is scope for State support to be applied in situations of extraordinary financial stress, the working assumption for future bank resolutions is that the bail-in of creditors, including bondholders, will be a first resort where banks are in trouble. But there is an implied hint in the new system that in times of serious systemic disruption of the banking system, there might be limits to the extent of the burden-sharing that would take place. Or as one European Commission memo puts it:

> The exact degree of burden-sharing would depend on the bank in question, the amount of losses that would need to be covered, and the wider economic situation ... where strictly necessary for financial stability, bail in could be discontinued upon reaching 8 per cent of total liabilities.[78]

So in the absence of a hard and fast rule, we will have to hope there are no real-life tests of the extent of burden-sharing in a major crisis.

But if something similar to the banking crisis that started in 2008 was to arise again in, say, 2020, it seems clear that the response would be quite different next time. Banking supervisors and policy makers should have more tools to work with, should be better prepared and should have a greater capacity to share costs with the private sector. New and different authorities will be making many of the key decisions. Perhaps even more importantly, the capital rules have been altered, so that the resilience of each institution against losses on its loan book ought to be considerably stronger. It is reasonable to hope that if the same set of circumstances were to arise in the European and Irish banking system again (and this is unlikely), the situation should be one where costs are less expensive for the Irish taxpayer to manage, and more broadly shared.

And there is reason to think, too, that better supervision and higher capital ratios, and the lessons of the past few years, will reduce the likelihood of banking crises happening in the first place. Let's hope so.

Where are we now?

On 28 November 2014, exactly four years after the Government announced that it had reached agreement and would accept an EU/IMF programme, the Minister for Finance, Michael Noonan, announced a programme of his own – this time to repay all of the IMF loans which Ireland had received, in a matter of months, and several years earlier than planned.

He was able to do so because a number of factors had come together to improve Ireland's position: interest rates for bonds worldwide had fallen hugely; Ireland's economic performance had improved considerably; unemployment had fallen very significantly; the economy was growing; and the banking sector was still fragile but no longer in intensive care.

The property market had first stabilised, then started to improve, allowing for huge asset sales by NAMA, reducing the risk that NAMA might cost the Government additional monies and increasing the likelihood that it will actually deliver some few billions back to the State over its lifetime. Ireland's balance of payments was healthy and its competitiveness in international trade and for foreign direct investment, after years of erosion in the period up to 2007, was now also on a much healthier track.

All of these improving indicators and a much more favourable market environment, greatly assisted by policy changes in the ECB, had led the bond market to invest more and more in Irish Government bonds. This was the same market, the same sort of investors, which had abandoned us in 2010. This process had started on 5 July 2012, when the first tentative steps were made by the NTMA to issue new Irish bonds back into that market. By that time, the NTMA had already persuaded investors to buy Irish government short-term paper, or in other words to lend us money for a period of a few weeks or months. But government bonds are loans that are not repaid for some years. There is a much bigger act of faith on the part of investors when they buy those. Now with the July bond issuance, there was evidence that faith was being restored, that the situation had started – but only started – to normalise.

By the time that the EU/IMF loan programme ended in December 2013 Ireland was so fully engaged once more with the bond markets that it had already managed to amass a very large pot of cash to finance the budget deficit for the coming year. This allowed the Minister for Finance to plan to exit the

EU/IMF programme without any backstop of support from the EU and IMF. That deficit was still expected, even after years of tax increases and big spending adjustments, to amount to 4¾ per cent of GDP, however – in cash terms, something around €8 billion. And the Government sector's debt at the start of the year was expected to be over €205 billion, or about 1¼ times the total earnings of the whole economy, as measured by GDP, in 2013.

The economy was now, finally, expected to grow by more than the paltry 0.2 per cent estimated outturns for 2012 and 2013. The Budget documentation reported that 'a modest recovery is taking hold in the Irish economy'. The expected growth rate for 2014 was 2 per cent, but by the time the 2015 Budget was being promulgated one year later, the expectation was that when all the counting was finished, 2014 would have produced a growth rate of not far off 5 per cent, with 3+ per cent growth rates expected for several years after that.[79]

Later, when Budget 2016 was promulgated in October 2015, Department of Finance figures estimated that growth in the economy – measured in GDP terms – would amount to over 6 per cent for 2015 and about 4.3 per cent in 2016. It was also expected that the Debt/GDP ratio, which is one measure of the affordability of the Government's debt, would fall to 93 per cent in 2016 and 87 per cent in 2018, after an end-year peak of around 120 per cent in 2012 and 2013. Debt levels were much improved, but still high enough to represent a risk factor for the economy.

By November 2015, the unemployment rate on a seasonally adjusted basis had fallen to just below 9 per cent from a peak of over 15 per cent in the depths of the crisis, but still well above the end 2007 level of 5 per cent.

By the end of 2015, property prices were into their third year of recovery, helping to improve the balance sheets of the banks who had extended loans against property and the businesses and individuals who had borrowed. Residential prices were still about a third down on the end-2007 level, but a good deal up on the low price levels reached in the depths of 2012. The Commercial Real Estate Sector was, in 2015, performing strongly in terms of prices and rents.

In the banking sector, too, we are clearly in a better phase. The decision of AIB Bank to start repaying Government capital at the end of 2015 is a symptom of this, as is the real improvement in the banks' arrears situation and their non-performing loans. Their profitability has been helped by write-backs, or reversals of provisions made for losses that did not arise. There remain challenges, including from a relatively muted underlying profit performance and a still too-high arrears level, remembering that for banks, profit allows capital to accumulate, making for stronger institutions.[80] The Irish banking system no longer requires huge funding from the central banking system – with Irish headquartered banks borrowing only around €10 billion from the Eurosystem at end-October 2015, according to the Central Bank.

It is hard to pick on a moment at which one could have finally said that the crisis phase was over for Ireland – not with those first tentative government bond sales in 2012, but certainly by the time the Government started to make repayments to the IMF one could say that Ireland was no longer in a national fiscal and economic crisis, even if for many individuals with high debt levels or mortgage arrears, or still unemployed after a very deep recession, the personal crisis might be ongoing.

For me, though, work on the Irish financial and economic crisis finished at the start of February 2012, when I resigned from the Department of Finance, after two years as Secretary General. A few months before, I had received a call from the Taoiseach, inviting me to accept the Government's nomination to the European Court of Auditors. The Court is exactly what it says – an audit body dealing with the audits of the European Union's activities. Each European member state nominates one of its nationals to be a member of the Court, and after a few controversial months, I joined the Court in March 2012, just before the NTMA managed to start issuing Irish paper again.

I am writing this section in November 2015 and I have not been at all involved in Irish public administration since early 2012, so there are current and more recent issues on which I am not in a position to comment. Still, I hope this book will provide an interesting reflection on some very important moments in our recent history.

Appendices

Text of the Government Announcement of the Bank Guarantee, 30 September 2008[81]

The Government has decided to put in place with immediate effect a guarantee arrangement to safeguard all deposits (retail, commercial, institutional and interbank), covered bonds, senior debt and dated subordinated debt (lower tier II), with the following banks: Allied Irish Bank, Bank of Ireland, Anglo Irish Bank, Irish Life and Permanent, Irish Nationwide Building Society and the Educational Building Society and such specific subsidiaries as may be approved by Government following consultation with the Central Bank and the Financial Regulator. It has done so following advice from the Governor of the Central Bank and the Financial Regulator about the impact of the recent international market turmoil on the Irish Banking system. The guarantee is being provided at a charge to the institutions concerned and will be subject to specific terms and conditions so that the taxpayers' interest can be protected. The guarantee will cover all existing aforementioned facilities with these institutions and any new such facilities issued from midnight on 29 September 2008, and will expire at midnight on 28 September 2010.

The decision has been taken by Government to remove any uncertainty on the part of counterparties and customers of the six credit institutions. The Government's objective in taking this decisive action is to maintain financial stability for the benefit of depositors and businesses and is in the best interests of the Irish economy.

The Financial Regulator has advised that all the financial institutions in Ireland will continue to be subject to normal on-going regulatory requirements.

This very important initiative by the Government is designed to safeguard the Irish financial system and to remedy a serious disturbance in the economy caused by the recent turmoil in the international financial markets.

Ends

On following pages are the text of letters between Jean-Claude Trichet of the ECB and Minister Brian Lenihan, October and November 2010.[82]

EUROPEAN CENTRAL BANK

EUROSYSTEM

__Strictly Confidential__

Jean-Claude TRICHET
President

Mr Brian Lenihan
Tánaiste and
Minister for Finance
Government Buildings
Upper Merrion Street
Dublin 2
Ireland

Frankfurt, 15 October 2010
L/JCT/10/1280

Dear Minister,

I refer to our last phone conversation. As you know the ECB greatly appreciates the recent commitment of the Irish government to develop, in close cooperation with the Commission in liaison with the ECB, a multi-annual economic and fiscal adjustment strategy. Given Ireland's convincing track-record in fiscal adjustment, I am confident that your medium-term strategy will be successful in restoring fiscal sustainability and financial sector soundness.

In this context, I would like to draw your attention to a number of issues arising from the *extraordinarily large provision of liquidity by the Eurosystem to Irish banks* in recent weeks. The participation in Eurosystem credit operations is subject to rules. These include the requirement for the Eurosystem to base its lending operations with market participants on adequate collateral. Moreover, the General Documentation on Eurosystem monetary policy instruments and procedures requires our counterparties to be financially sound. In this context, the Eurosystem may limit, exclude or suspend counterparties' access to monetary policy instruments on the grounds of prudence and may reject or limit the use of assets in the Eurosystem credit operations by specific counterparties. The Governing Council indeed carefully monitors the Eurosystem credit granted to the banking system, in the Irish as well as in all other cases, and in particular the size of Eurosystem exposures to individual banks, the financial soundness of these banks, and the collateral they provide to the Eurosystem. The assessment by the Governing Council of the appropriateness of its exposures to Irish banks depends very much on progress in economic policy adjustment, enhancing financial sector capital and bank restructuring.

Kaiserstrasse 29, 60311 Frankfurt am Main, Germany · Tel.: +49 69 13 44 73 00 · Fax: +49 69 13 44 73 05

2

Moreover, the provision of *Emergency Liquidity Assistance (ELA)* by the Central Bank of Ireland, as by any other National Central Bank of the Eurosystem, is closely monitored by the ECB's Governing Council as it may interfere with the objectives and tasks of the Eurosystem and the prohibition of monetary financing under the Treaties. Therefore, if ELA is provided in significant amounts, the Governing Council will assess whether there is a need to impose specific conditions in order to protect the integrity of our monetary policy. In addition, in order to ensure compliance with the monetary financing prohibition, it is essential to ensure that the ELA recipient institution continues to be solvent.

Against the background of these principles, I would like to re-emphasize that the current *large provision of liquidity by the Eurosystem and the Central Bank of Ireland to entities such as Anglo Irish Bank should not be taken for granted as a long-term solution.* Given these principles, the Governing Council cannot commit to maintaining the size of its funding to these institutions on a permanent basis.

As I told you, a key element of the monitoring by the Governing Council of Eurosystem exposure to the Irish banking system, and the related decisions the Governing Council may take, will be its assessment of *progress in implementing the four-year economic strategy* that the Irish government envisages to announce in early November. This is not only because significant parts of the Irish banking systems are partially or fully Government owned, but also because an important share of the Eurosystem exposure to Irish credit institutions is collateralised with securities issued or guaranteed by the Irish Government. I trust that the four-year strategy will target a fiscal deficit of below 3% in 2014 and a decline in the public debt-to-GDP ratio from 2012/13 onward, based on cautious real growth forecasts, as well as a strong structural reform programme. Future decisions by the Governing Council of the ECB regarding the terms of liquidity provision to Irish banks will thus need to take into account appropriate progress in the areas of fiscal consolidation, structural reforms and financial sector restructuring.

With my best regards,

Cc.:   Mr Olli Rehn, EU Commissioner for Economic and Monetary Affairs
        Mr Joaquín Almunia, EU Commissioner for Competition

An Roinn Airgeadais **Oifig an Aire**
Department of Finance **Office of the Minister**

Sráid Mhuirfean Uacht,	Upper Merrion Street,	Teileafón / Telephone: 353-1 604 5626
Baile Átha Cliath 2,	Dublin 2,	Facsuimhir / Facsimile: 353-1 676 1951
Éire.	Ireland.	Glao Áitiúil / LoCall: 1890 66 10 10
		http://www.finance.gov.ie

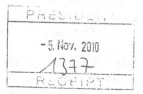

Mr Jean Claude Trichet
President
European Central Bank
Kaiserstrasse 29
60311 Frankfurt am Main
Germany

4 November, 2010.

Dear President,

You will no doubt have noted the very adverse developments in the markets in recent days in relation to the widening spread of Irish Government bonds against the German bund. This issue gives rise to very serious concerns for the Irish Government particularly in relation to the potential impact on the credibility of the very significant budgetary adjustments which we have developed working closely with the European authorities. I know that this concern is one that is strongly shared by you.

The increase in spreads is of course underpinned by a variety of factors. International concerns regarding the budgetary and banking position in Ireland have for some months contributed to a situation where Irish spreads were consistently higher than those in most other Member States. As you know the Irish authorities are embarking on a significant continuation and intensification of our policy actions to achieve budgetary sustainability. It is absolutely vital that these endeavours are successful in order to secure fiscal and, indeed, overall financial stability in Ireland.

Páipéar 100% Athchúrsáilte
Printed on 100% recycled paper

1

However, it is very noticeable that over recent days the widening in spreads has accelerated on the basis of speculation on the conditions that may be necessary to apply to the debt of countries accessing the European Financial Stability Facility and reported policy comments of senior political figures. It is the case that many market commentators attribute these comments as being the primary driver of the increased spreads of peripheral countries, including Ireland, in recent days.

I fully appreciate that there are valid legitimate policy perspectives for individual Member States to hold and disclose but the reality is that already difficult market conditions are being worsened.

I am sure that you will agree that it imperative that comments particularly from senior political figures within the eurozone are consistent in their content and do not, as an unintended consequence, undermine the efforts of Member States such as Ireland to address the serious difficulties that they are continuing to confront.

I hope you agree with me on this matter and will continue to use your influence to help calm markets.

I enclose for reference some press commentary from recent days in both domestic and international media on this point as well as the latest details on the spreads of 10 year Government bonds in Ireland and other peripheral eurozone countries.

Yours sincerely,

Brian Lenihan TD,
Minister for Finance

EUROPEAN CENTRAL BANK

EUROSYSTEM

Jean-Claude TRICHET
President

Mr Brian Lenihan
Tánaiste and
Minister of Finance
Government Buildings
Upper Merrion Street
Dublin 2
Ireland

Frankfurt, 19 November 2010
L/JCT/10/1444

Dear Minister,

As you are aware from my previous letter dated 15 October, the provision of *Emergency Liquidity Assistance (ELA)* by the Central Bank of Ireland, as by any other national central bank of the Eurosystem, is closely monitored by the Governing Council of the European Central Bank (ECB) as it may interfere with the objectives and tasks of the Eurosystem and may contravene the prohibition of monetary financing. Therefore, whenever ELA is provided in significant amounts, the Governing Council needs to assess whether it is appropriate to impose specific conditions in order to protect the integrity of our monetary policy. In addition, in order to ensure compliance with the prohibition of monetary financing, it is essential to ensure that ELA recipient institutions continue to be solvent.

As I indicated at the recent Eurogroup meeting, the exposure of the Eurosystem and of the Central Bank of Ireland vis-à-vis Irish financial institutions has risen significantly over the past few months to levels that we consider with great concern. Recent developments can only add to these concerns. As Patrick Honohan knows, the Governing Council has been asked yesterday to authorise new liquidity assistance which it did.

But all these considerations have implications for the assessment of the solvency of the institutions which are currently receiving ELA. It is the position of the Governing Council that it is only if we receive in writing a commitment from the Irish Government vis-à-vis the Eurosystem on the four following points that we can authorise further provisions of ELA to Irish financial institutions:

1)   The Irish government shall send a request for financial support to the Eurogroup;

2)   The request shall include the commitment to undertake decisive actions in the areas of fiscal consolidation, structural reforms and financial sector restructuring, in agreement with the European Commission, the International Monetary Fund and the ECB;

2

3)   The plan for the restructuring of the Irish financial sector shall include the provision of the necessary capital to those Irish banks needing it and will be funded by the financial resources provided at the European and international level to the Irish government as well as by financial means currently available to the Irish government, including existing cash reserves of the Irish government;

4)   The repayment of the funds provided in the form of ELA shall be fully guaranteed by the Irish Government, which would ensure the payment of immediate compensation to the Central Bank of Ireland in the event of missed payments on the side of the recipient institutions.

I am sure that you are aware that a swift response is needed before markets open next week, as evidenced by recent market tensions which may further escalate, possibly in a disruptive way, if no concrete action is taken by the Irish government on the points I mention above.

Besides the issue of the provision of ELA, the Governing Council of the ECB is extremely concerned about the very large overall credit exposure of the Eurosystem towards the Irish banking system. The Governing Council constantly monitors the credit granted to the banking system not only in Ireland but in all euro area countries, and in particular the size of Eurosystem exposures to individual banks, the financial soundness of these banks and the collateral they provide to the Eurosystem. The assessment of the Governing Council on the appropriateness of the Eurosystem's exposure to Irish banks will essentially depend on rapid and decisive progress in the formulation of a concrete action plan in the areas which have been mentioned in this letter and in its subsequent implementation.

With kind regards

Cc.: Mr Brian Cowen, Prime Minister

An Roinn Airgeadais   **Oifig an Aire**
Department of Finance   **Office of the Minister**

Sráid Mhuirfean Uacht,	Upper Merrion Street,	Teileafón / Telephone: 353-1 604 562●
Baile Átha Cliath 2,	Dublin 2,	Facsuimhir / Facsimile: 353-1 676 195?
Éire.	Ireland.	Glao Áitiúil / LoCall: 1890 66 10 10
		http://www.finance.gov.ie

21 November 2010

M. Jean-Claude Trichet
President
European Central Bank
Kaiserstrasse 29
60311 Frankfurt am Main
Germany

Dear Jean-Claude

I refer to your letter of 19 November 2010.

First, let me say that I fully understand your concerns and that of the Governing Council in regard to the implications of the current situation of the Irish banking system. As you know, Ireland has worked very aggressively, and to the limits of our fiscal capacity, to protect and repair the banking system in the light of the dangers to financial stability both in Ireland and Europe.

For example, in September 2008 the Government introduced an extensive Bank Guarantee to seek to bolster the funding difficulties of the banks by providing a Sovereign guarantee of bank liabilities. This was quickly followed by a bank recapitalisation programme announced in December 2008 and nationalisation of Anglo Irish Bank in January 2009. The establishment of NAMA was announced in April 2009 to remove the riskiest land and property development loans from the banks' balance sheets. At this stage, Ireland has provided or pledged some €32 billion of capital to the banking system.

These extensive set of measures have been taken in tandem with a most extensive programme of fiscal adjustment, amounting to some €15 billion of discretionary fiscal consolidation in 2009 and 2010 so far, with a further adjustment of another €15 billion planned by 2014. Measures for 2011 alone will amount to over €6 billion. Thus, Ireland has proved so far to be flexible and aggressive in dealing with its problems and will continue to be so.

258

These assertive measures, contributed to a substantial improvement in international sentiment towards Ireland and a partial recovery in the banks' funding position in the first quarter of 2010. The new Financial Regulator announced the results of his PCAR exercise and required the banks to meet it by the end of the year. The banks successfully commenced the process of accessing longer-term funding to manage the large redemptions cliff due in September. Reliance on bank funding from the Eurosystem was reduced. In addition, Bank of Ireland initiated and ultimately successfully completed its private capital raising exercise.

However it was not possible to sustain the improvement in the banking environment. As the year progressed there were a number of developments which led to a sharp reversal in financial conditions, of which the following are just some.

- Following the onset of the Greek debt crisis during April, international markets became increasingly concerned regarding Ireland's fiscal position, the strength of the Bank Guarantee and the fiscal capacity of the State to stand behind the banks.
- There was a slowdown in the pace of economic recovery nationally and increasing concern regarding the speed of recovery in the international economy particularly in the USA.
- Credit rating actions and negative market sentiment exacerbated the situation
- Uncertainty about the status of bondholders in the event of access to external support added to instability
- These events led to a crisis of confidence in both the Irish banking system and increasingly the Irish Sovereign. As a result, our banks, as you know so well, have had to turn to ECB/Central Bank funding to replace their market funding especially in September when a large number of bonds which matured under the two year Credit Institutions Financial Support (CIFS) Guarantee became due.

In order to seek to reverse these trends, I made a further comprehensive and detailed further Statement on Banking at the end of September and outlined the actions being taken to provide certainty to the international markets on the scale of bank losses. The Statement covered changes to NAMA to accelerate loan transfers and provide visibility on the final discounts expected to arise, the revised assessment of the capital positions of the banks on the basis of final expected NAMA discounts and the projected maximum capital requirements for Anglo Irish Bank.

While initially this information was initially well received, the credibility of projected bank loan losses was increasingly called into question by analysts and investors – there comes a point at which negative sentiment starts to feed on itself, even independently of underlying realities, and we are clearly at that point.

In relation to points (1) to (4) of your letter, I would like to inform you that the Irish Government has decided today to seek access to external support from the European and international support mechanisms. This grave and serious decision has been taken in the light of the developments I have outlined above and informed by your recent communications, and the advice you have conveyed to me personally and courteously in recent days.

The Government is clear, in the light of the very intensive and productive work done by Irish, European Commission, IMF and of course ECB officials, in recent days, that there is a potential programme which will be both workable and effective and which will incorporate real and significant restructuring measures in relation to the financial sector, structural reforms and fiscal consolidation, and the Government is committed to this. Indeed, your officials in Dublin have had the opportunity to see a draft of our proposed four year plan, so you may be aware that our fiscal and economic programme is in fact very extensive, and forms an appropriate basis for programme discussions.

It is also clear from the discussions over recent days that any programme will include provision for further capitalisation on a scale which should convince markets that capital is not a problem. I was very pleased to note that the intensive examination of the Irish authorities' work on capital requirements has not indicated any new and unanticipated 'hole' in the banks' capital position, and it would be helpful if this is made clear in internal and external communications. However, the fact is that the market has not accepted the current capital levels as adequate, so more must be done.

In relation to your fourth point, there are already such arrangements in place in respect of each bank in receipt of ELA which provide the assurances that you call for.

I hope that this will provide some reassurance to the Governing Council and that you will be able to reiterate in a public way the continuing practical support of the ECB for the liquidity position of the Irish banks, to help to reassure the market on this crucial point.

You know that we here will not be lacking in the will to do all that is necessary on our part to protect our economy and people and to play our role in the Eurosystem.

Yours sincerely

Brian Lenihan, TD
Minister for Finance

Endnotes

Chapter 1

1 INBS had a peculiarity that required some consideration – its branches opened on a Saturday morning. It was hoped that any intervention could be managed over a weekend, but if the media or the public noticed that large teams of staff were known to be working over a Friday night, then there was the added danger of a panic at the branches on a Saturday morning.

2 Hank Paulson described it thus: 'By mid-September, after 13 months of market stress, the financial system essentially seized up and we had a system-wide crisis. Credit markets froze and banks substantially reduced interbank lending. Confidence was seriously compromised throughout our financial system. Our system was on the verge of collapse, a collapse that would have significantly worsened and prolonged the economic downturn that was already underway.' (Speech at the Ronald Reagan Presidential Library, 20 November 2008)

3 The British Bank that had been rescued by the UK authorities after a very public bank run the previous year.

4. The relevant extract of David McWilliams book *Follow the Money* was published in the *Irish Independent* on 31 October 2009, and is available on www.independent.ie, as of end-December 2015.

5 The commission had to come from the independent Central Bank and financial regulator, as they had access rights to the banks that the Department of Finance and NTMA never enjoyed, but my NTMA colleagues and I had strongly encouraged the regulator to take this initiative. The results were shared among the authorities and the Dame Street people were pragmatic in ensuring that everyone who needed access to the data could get it. A few months before,

this would have been anathema.

6 Article entitled 'State guarantees can avert depression', *Sunday Business Post*, 28 September 2008

7 In other words of packaging loans into a legal structure that could be acceptable under central banking rules as collateral, thus allowing ILP to borrow more from the ECB

8 i.e. HRE.

Chapter 2

9 In his evidence to the Oireachtas Banking Inquiry on 8 July 2015, available online (as of end-August 2015) at https://inquiries.oireach-tas.ie/banking/hearings/

10 Evidence given on 29 July and available online (as of end-August 2015) at https://inquiries.oireachtas.ie/banking/hearings/

11 When banks issue bonds, they are in effect issuing a promise to pay interest over a pre-determined period of time, at the end of which they will repay the capital sum of the loan itself. In the event that a bank would have to be liquidated, the bondholders normally have the same right to be repaid as the bulk of other unsecured creditors, out of the assets of the bank. In relation to subordinated bonds, things are different. These creditors get paid only after the ordinary creditors including 'senior' bondholders are paid. If there is a shortage of assets they get paid less, or nothing. Subordinated debt is therefore regarded as a more risky investment and the investors get a higher interest rate to reflect that. If an investor believes that the chance of a bank failure is very low, they will happily invest in the subordinated debt and enjoy the higher returns.

12 Federal Deposit Insurance Corporation.

13 Some subordinated debt has a fixed date or range of dates when repayment falls due (dated subordinated debt) whereas some carry no fixed date for repayment. Sometimes this can be referred to as 'perpetual' debt, because the bank can continue paying interest and repaying no part of the capital amount indefinitely. Generally, the bank may decide to repay if it wishes.

14 Much study had been done of the Commission's approach to the Northern Rock case, which suggested they might, relatively speaking, 'go easy' on a liquidity guarantee with a charge to the institution concerned.

15 This required a discussion with the AIB and Bank of Ireland people present in the building about the contribution they could make, now that Anglo was to be guaranteed, to ensuring any shortfall the next day could be met. (It is clear from my notes that Bank of Ireland in particular was very reluctant to provide any liquidity to Anglo for more than a very short period, if even that). It also entailed further arrangements among the authorities.

Chapter 3

16 Finance Spokesperson for the Labour Party, becoming a Minister, then Tánaiste (Deputy Prime Minister) in the subsequent Government.

17 Then head of the biggest opposition party, Fine Gael, later Taoiseach (Prime Minister).

18 Then French Finance Minister and Chair of the Council of Finance Ministers (ECOFIN) of the European Union, later President of the IMF.

19 As indicated, European Commissioner dealing with competition and state aids.

20 Then Britain's Finance Minister, the Chancellor of the Exchequer.

21 The Irish and UK authorities later instituted a 'Cross Border Stability Group' which met regularly by teleconference to ensure coordination and information flow. While we on the Irish side sometimes thought the information flow was a bit one-sided (maybe the UK felt the same), we did manage to avoid subsequent bust-ups and had a much more positive and cooperative approach to mutual issues than might otherwise have been the case. The prior existence of such a forum might, but only might, have been helpful in September 2008.

22 This too was addressed later with the institution of a *'cellule de crise'* – a group of grandees available to deal with imminent crises, supported by a central phone line that one would call when big events were likely to happen. We used that line religiously over the next year or so when making significant banking announcements, but I suspect it fell into disuse as more informal arrangements arose.

23 The other important business of the day was to seek to ensure that no statements were made from the ECOFIN that would undermine Irish efforts and to reach out to Commissioners Kroes and Almunia – in that regard the day was not without its hiccoughs.

24 Darling's own account of the financial crisis (*Back from the Brink*, Atlantic Books, 2011) gives a fascinating account of this very difficult day for the UK authorities.

25 One addition – Postbank – a then new joint venture between the Post Office and a foreign bank was agreed.

Chapter 4

26 The *cellule de crise* – see footnote 22.

Chapter 5

27 Email of 15 October 2008 from the author to senior staff in the Central Bank, Financial Regulator, NTMA, Department of Finance, and office of the Attorney General, as well as to Arthur Cox solicitors.

28 At the time of writing, the author may yet be asked to act as a witness in relation to various criminal or civil cases, and has therefore decided not to deal here with a number of important issues in relation to Anglo Irish bank and the Irish Life and Permanent group.

29 He did not rule out raising capital by means of sales of AIB assets – the sale of AIB's stake in US based M&T bank was often suggested as one way in which AIB could raise funds, but it also owned a large stake in a substantial Polish bank. This stake, too, was eventually sold to release capital for AIB.

30 Allied Irish Banks PLC Interim Management Statement of 5 November 2008.

31 Government Announcement on Recapitalisation of Banks, 21 December 2008, available as of end-August 2015 at http://finance.gov.ie/news-centre/press-releases/government-announcement-recapitalisation-21st-december-2008.

32 Includes EBS, the building society which was subsumed into AIB.

33 The annual report of the National Pension Reserve Fund is available (as of end-August 2015) at http://nprf.ie/Publications/2015/AnnualReport2014.pdf.

34 Article titled 'I'll Probably Punch Lenihan' – Drumm' by Tom Lyons and Gavin Sheridan.

35 These and other issues are already widely discussed in the public domain – some of that discussion has led me to issue legal proceedings or obtain apologies or corrections, when my own role was misrepresented in newspapers and books.

36 http://www.centralbank.ie/press-area/press-releases/Pages/State-mentbyAuthority.aspx.

Chapter 7

37 From Dr Somers' evidence to the Oireachtas Banking Inquiry of 10 July 2015, available as of end-august 2015 from https://inquiries.oireachtas.ie/banking/hearings/

38 In the *Irish Independent*, 16 March 2012, full title 'Brendan Mc-Donagh: Busting NAMA myths – interests of taxpayers are at core of agency'.

Chapter 9

39 In a transcript of an interview with journalists Brian Blackstone and Matthew Karnitschnig of the *Wall Street Journal*, 26 January 2010 and available (as of end-August 2015) online at http://www.wsj.com/articles/SB10001424052748703906204575027064001835410.

40 A specialist in applying mathematical and statistical techniques to economic problems.

Chapter 10

41 The Executive Board consists of the President of the ECB (then Mr Trichet, now Mr Draghi), a vice-President and four other members. Between them they are responsible for the day to day management of the ECB.

Chapter 11

42 Letters to two prime ministers' is available online at http://asia.nikkei.com/Features/Jean-Claude-Trichet/Jean-Claude-Trichet-24-Letters-to-two-prime-ministers as of end-August 2015).

43 For example, Ashoka Mody's article entitled 'The Ghost of Deau-ville' of 7 January 2014 and available as of mid-September 2015 at http://www.voxeu.org/article/ghost-deauville.

44 About €4 billion net for the four weeks to 29 October, for the banks being supported by the Irish Government.

45 Masuch told me that the ECB needed a very convincing overall package such that they could be sure about good prospects for debt sustainability and bank solvency and – based on this – could continue with flexible liquidity support to Irish banks as long as this was needed. And indeed, in fairness to him, once banks were recapi-

talised and the fiscal adjustment was on track, Masuch did support the Irish case in public, arguing for example that Irish sovereign debt was sustainable, when others were not convinced about this assessment.

46 For a rejection of ELA a two-third majority in the Governing Council of the ECB is needed.

47 There were of course days and weeks when there were inflows also, but the net trend had been consistently negative.

Chapter 12

48 As I write this it strikes me that over the course of the crisis our concept of time had changed. Events and decisions that in normal times would have been the most momentous of any civil servants' working year are now hard to bring to mind, because they paled into insignificance beside other much more momentous events. And the timescale for decisions became amazingly short – huge amounts of work were being concentrated into very short periods, a great deal could be done in three weeks, and near disasters could emerge in hours or days.

49 Although ironically there was an initial reduction in bond yields on the putative news of the bailout.

Chapter 13

50 This was not a great shock. The sheer scale of the liquidity needs of the banks was so large that one really needed the ability to 'print money' to meet that demand – only the ECB could do this and the other EU support facilities and the IMF each had limits – they had to conserve some firepower for other potential troubled cases.

51 Their logic was that a programme was probably needed to ensure that banks would be sufficiently recapitalised and debt sustainability ensured so that Irish government securities could continue to be accepted as adequate collateral from the ECB perspective.

52 Nor was it coming from the ECB, incidentally.

53 From Statement of the Eurogroup on Ireland, 16 November 2010 (text available as of end-August 2015, from http://www.consilium. europa.eu/en/press/press-releases/?stDt=20101116).

54 The Troika parties seemed comfortable dealing with their Irish colleagues. At some point Masuch, for example, told me that he was impressed by the quality of our staff and the efficient organisation of

the negotiation process. This certainly helped to convince the ECB team that our commitments made were credible and we had full ownership.

Chapter 14

55 Some of the information was stark – the memo noted that the banking system had lost €133 billion of market and deposit funding since the beginning of 2010, of which €85 billion had arisen in 2010. The banks were now relying on central bank funding to the tune of €118 billion, €35 billion of which was emergency liquidity assistance from the Central Bank of Ireland and the rest directly from the ECB. Bank of Ireland and AIB had both had to rely for some of their financing on ELA.

56 It was the existence of this cash stockpile that had allowed the Government to take some time over its decision to seek outside support.

57 Working out the likely interest rate was complicated enough. There were different regimes for each of the facilities concerned, so that the mix of funding as between the various facilities made some difference, and any funds received at variable interest rates would be 'swapped' in financial markets for fixed rate funds, by the NTMA, which would add to the interest cost, albeit with the benefit of additional stability.

58 Statement to the Oireachtas Joint Committee on Economic Regulatory Affairs, 6 October 2010.

59 There had been a small experiment in senior bond burden-sharing earlier in the crisis period. Irish Nationwide offered at one stage to buy back senior bonds from the market at the reduced price at which they were then trading. The amounts were small and no bondholder was going to be forced to take the deal, but the reaction from Moody's credit rating agency was swift. They came very close to downgrading the whole Irish banking system, on the basis that any wavering in the Government's support to the system and its creditors, even on such a voluntary basis, would be tantamount to a declaration that all bondholders could expect to make losses. That the initiative was the building society's not the Government's made no difference. This position was somewhat surprising, but indicated the extent to which any burden-sharing with senior bondholders might be expected to 'shock' the market.

60   In an interview for a German documentary entitled 'The Secret Bank Bailout', available on YouTube, Jörg Asmussen, at the time of the interview speaking as an ECB Executive Board member, said that the ECB 'saw the dangers of contagion' and that it was 'a priority objective to prevent the contagion'. But at the time the ECB had also stressed that 'burning' of senior bank bondholders could also undermine financial stability *in Ireland*.

Chapter 16

61 Programme documents are available at http://www.finance.gov. ie/what-we-do/eu-international/irelands-programme-eu-imf-programme, and the specific documents agreed in discussions at the end of November 2010, and finalised and ratified as appropriate in early December 2010 are available at http://www.finance.gov.ie/ sites/default/files/euimfrevised.pdf (as of end-August 2015).

62 It had been formed a few months earlier, over the course of a very short number of weeks, as a Luxembourg company. In other words, it was not even a part of the European Union framework, but rather was a vehicle established by the Eurozone member states for the specific purpose of borrowing and lending to crisis countries. It was, so, an infant in age terms, and an orphan in institutional terms. Being new, it was also very small. The initial bond issues were managed by an EFSF with a staff of only a handful of people.

63 This is based on the expected interest rate on EU/IMF funds (swapped to fixed rate) at the start of the programme; I have not tried to calculate an effective marginal rate at the point where capital was actually injected.

64 As I understand, Eurostat rules have since been changed in a way which had it been applied to Irish statistics at the time, would have been very unhelpful. A useful paper on statistical treatment of bank rescues is available in the ECB Statistical Papers Series – No. 7/April 2015.

Chapter 17

65 This would not cause a huge delay, as the assessment was due to be completed by the end of the month.

66 In the end, and with the cooperation of the ECB, this is what happened.

67 At least this Franco-German approach was done in a transparent way. There were various – thankfully only relatively few – attempts to use our weakened financial position to make extortionate demands during the crisis.

Chapter 18

68 As with all the previous banking announcements, this one risked being dogged by difficult external circumstances – John Corrigan, for example, reported on the Friday that Standard and Poor's might make a further downgrading of Ireland even before the announcement the following Thursday.

69 The note entitled 'Irish Letters' is available from the ECB website (as of end-August 2015) at http://www.ecb.europa.eu/press/html/irish-letters.en.html.

70 Irish diplomats in Washington were able to hear what was being said to members of Congress through their own contacts.

71 This same outfit have recently been fighting hard – and it seems winning – in the US courts in an effort to force the Argentinian government to pay more to them than to other bondholders.

Afterword

72 Transcript of oral evidence given to the Banking Inquiry on 10 September 2015 by Ajai Chopra is available (as of mid-September 2015) on https://inquiries.oireachtas.ie/banking/hearings/

73 Transcript of oral evidence given to the Banking Inquiry on 10 September 2015 by Michael Noonan is available (as of mid-September 2015) on https://inquiries.oireachtas.ie/banking/hearings/

74 The December 2010 report (though not published until 1 March 2011) is formally entitled 'Strengthening the Capacity of the Department of Finance – Report of the Independent Review Panel' and is available (as of mid-September 2015) from http://oldwww.finance.gov.ie/documents/publications/reports/2011/deptreview.pdf. It was prepared by Rob Wright, a former Deputy Minister of the Canadian Department of Finance, Hans Borstlap, a highly experienced Dutch official and John Malone, formerly Secretary General of the Department of Agriculture, with support from economist Pat McArdle.

75 Despite an earlier scepticism on the part of Minister Lenihan, this idea made its way into the Government's four year plan – the 'National Recovery Plan' of November 2010: available as of mid-Sep-

tember 2015 from http://www.budget.gov.ie.

76 I tried a number of times to persuade Minister Lenihan to publish earlier, but he would not budge – he argued that earlier publication would be taken as a political manoeuvre in advance of the election. I was anxious that the report would be available to the opposition as they prepared their policies on the public service, and was concerned that the Department's staff should not be left in the dark about something so important to them. Later some conspiracy theorist or other posited that the timing of the publication was some sort of political tactic on the part of the Department itself – not so: we published it as soon as we were let.

77 'Council Adopts Rules Setting up Single Resolution Mechanism', press release of the Council of the European Union dated 14 July 2014.

78 European Commission memo entitled 'EU Bank Recovery and Resolution Directive (BRRD): Frequently Asked Questions' dated 5 April 2014 and available as of mid-September 2015 from http://europa.eu/rapid/press-release_MEMO-14-297_en.htm.

79 All of these numbers were later revised – at the end of July 2015, 2014 GDP growth was estimated by the Central Statistics Office at 5.2 per cent, and GNP growth at nearly 7 per cent, among the strongest performances in Europe.

80 The Central Bank's Macro Financial Review of December 2015 outlines the position of the economy and the banks available as of end-December 2015 at http://www.centralbank.ie/publications. Other data sources for this section of this book include the Department of Finance, NTMA and Central Statistics Office websites.

Appendices

81. Department of Finance website – available as of end-August 2015 from http://finance.gov.ie/sites/default/files/blo11_0.pdf.

82. ECB website, available as of end-August 2015 at http://www.ecb.europa.eu/press/html/irish-letters.en.html.

Index

271

Index